PASTORAL COUNSELING
AND SPIRITUAL VALUES

PASTORAL COUNSELING AND SPIRITUAL VALUES:

A BLACK POINT OF VIEW

Edward P. Wimberly

ABINGDON • Nashville

PASTORAL COUNSELING AND SPIRITUAL VALUES:
A BLACK POINT OF VIEW
Copyright © 1982 by Abingdon

Library of Congress Cataloging in Publication Data
WIMBERLY, EDWARD P., 1943-
  Pastoral counseling and spiritual values.
  Includes bibliographical references.
  1. Pastoral counseling. I. Title.
  BV4012.2.W49   253.5'08996073   81-10918   AACR2

ISBN 0-687-30336-2

Scripture quotations are from the Revised Standard Version of the Bible,
copyrighted 1946, 1952, © 1971, 1973 by the Division of Christian
Education of the National Council of the Churches of Christ in the U.S.A.,
and are used by permission.

Chapter 3 is adapted from Edward P. Wimberly's "Holism in the Family:
Implications for the Church from a Jungian Perspective," *Pastoral
Psychology* vol. 28 (Spring 1980). Used by permission.

MANUFACTURED BY THE PARTHENON PRESS AT
NASHVILLE, TENNESSEE, UNITED STATES OF AMERICA

To

Thomas J. Pugh
and The Interdenominational Theological Center:
Pioneers in pastoral counseling in the black community

CONTENTS

PREFACE

Pastoral counseling is becoming, and will become, increasingly important for black Christians. The reason for this is found in he impact that technological society has had upon black religious tradition. Fundamentally, modern society is characterized by a transformation socially, politically, psychologically, and religiously, brought about by technology and reflecting the uprooting of beliefs and values from modern life.[1] Our contemporary world has peculiar, distinctive qualities that emphasize private selection of values. People choose their own values from a variety of competing sources.[2] Another phenomenon of the modern period is what many sociologists have called secularism, which is the exclusion of all religious references from our common life. Although life goes on with a great deal of continuity within the black community, we are now under attack by the pervasive social and economic forces of the present. Many of the support structures and traditions of the black church, which have been conveyers and custodians of past cherished values, are now feeling the slicing cut of the sharp blades of modern progress. We are stumbling into an era when traditional values will have less impact upon our lives as individuals, even when we remain vigilant to preserve these values.

9

Perhaps the three most important historical movements in the black community that highlight the impact of technological culture on this community are the black power movement, the black awareness movement, and the cult movement. All three movements are contextual and reflect a response to the modernization set in motion by technology. For example, the new self-awareness orientation in the black community, emphasizing a new appreciation of black pigmentation as well as inherent characteristics and potentials in the black psyche for self-actualization, emerged at a time when the demands of melting-pot conformism became a real threat.[3] Modern technological society cannot comfortably deal with persons as unique entities nor with pluralistic ethnic identities; scientific technological society pushes for generalities rather than particulars, categories of sameness rather than unique differences. Statistical analysis, a common tool of modern thought, can quantify on the basis of likeness, and this penchant for likeness dominates the wider cultural value orientation. Therefore, black awareness is a resistant response to the coercive tendencies of uniformity.

Another response to the influence of modernization is the black power movement. It is an attempt to slow down the process of amalgamation into the melting pot through political and economic means of community control. It is a response to the government and society's attempt to systematize, homogenize, and generalize. The motto of this movement is "hold on to and control your own identity and institutions."

Perhaps the most threatening aspect of modernity is the impact that the scientific world-view is having, and will have, upon the traditions of the black church. The scientific world-view is secular; it pushes all transcendent interpretations of reality aside and attempts to reduce all views of reality to what is observable and measurable. One effect of such a value orientation is to limit one's striving for truth, the good and ultimate reality, to the material world of observable and measurable. Proponents of this scientism urge people to abandon their traditional beliefs and to think that their salvation rests in the liberation from these old religious ideas. Although scientism has attacked the icons of faith, and is touted as a new expression of the search for the ultimate, it does not help people meet their needs for something beyond themselves. Rather, it tends to push people toward denying the need for the transcendent.

The rapid rise of cultism in America, particularly in the black community, is the clearest example of the failure of the scientific world-view to respond to the seeker's need for the ultimate. If persons do not have a God in heaven who loves and cares for them, they will find a substitute on earth who will be totally incapable of lifting persons out of the conditions of their existence. Cultism has emerged in the black community primarily because liberal black Protestantism has bought into the secularistic ideology of this worldliness and has lost sight of the real need for the transcendent. The this-worldly orientation, although a healthy corrective to escapist other-worldly orientations, has gone to the extreme of denying the other-worldly dimension and its interpenetration with this world.

The above analysis is included to lift up the moral and spiritual context to which a ministry of pastoral counseling must respond. It must carry out its function and task in a society where people are frantically in need of emotional, moral, and spiritual direction, particularly when the dominant cultural world-view offers little help. While it is very urgent that we try to hold on to traditional values that are embodied in our religious heritage, the cultural value system we live in will be putting great pressure on individuals and families to shape their own religious, moral, and emotional lives without the help of tradition. To respond to this phenomenon, more attention will need to be given to people and families with the intent to help them shape their spiritual, moral, and emotional lives. This is the way pastoral counseling, as one response to modernity, can play an important role. As tradition loses its grip upon the lives of individuals, more specialized focus will need to be given to people to help replace the moral and spiritual role that culture and traditional patterns once played.

This picture painted here is not a prediction of the demise of the black church tradition. Rather, it is a call to the black church to pay close attention to the needs of people as individuals and as small families. The ministry of the future will have to be holistic, and give specific attention to people and their needs outside the traditional morning worship. The skills of a pastoral counselor and group counselor will become more apparent as tradition loses its hold on black persons, and supportive ministries to supplement the worship service are needed.

In order to help the black church respond to people's needs in the future through pastoral counseling, the theory of depth psychology should *not* be ignored. However, this theoretical model by itself has severe limitations and restricted relevance for black Christians and the black church. But when the norms from the black Christian experience are applied to a depth psychological perspective, depth psychology takes on a new significance and relevance for pastoral counseling with black Christians in a technological age. This work seeks to apply the norm of the unity of all experience growing out of Afro-American roots to depth psychology as well as to other behavioral science theories. The unity-of-experience theme is the organizing principle of the book and will be applied as well to humanistic systems theory, family systems theory, and Jungian psychology. Here, *unity of experience* refers to the idea that reality is essentially a whole, and that people, society, institutions, the spiritual realm, and nature are interpenetrating and interacting entities significantly related to each other.

I wrote this book partly to continue the work started in my first publication, *Pastoral Care in the Black Church*. After discussing that book with others, there appeared to me to be some dimensions that needed to be pursued in more detail. This particularly is true with regard to the healing aspect of pastoral counseling with reference to depth psychology and the spiritual perspective.

Another reason for writing this book is to respond to the criticism that in the first book I used Euro-American theories and categories for developing my ideas. This criticism is accurate; however, it misses the essence of what I understand as blackness. To my way of thinking, blackness refers to an in-depth exploration of one's own history of socialization, family history, racial and religious history, and one's biological endowment; it further refers to owning and befriending all these various dimensions of one's autobiographical and biological history, including the negative as well as the positive; it also means recognition of the fact that, in varied degrees of influence, part of our heritage has been affected by interaction with Euro-American influences as well as Afro-American dimensions. Once one has befriended, explored, and owned one's biographical and biological history, one must achieve a real identity by integrating the conscious and unconscious aspects of these dimensions into a unity that participates in, as well as transcends, the contributory antecedents. In this way, you and I become the organizing principle around which our identities are formed. We are not just passive participants in shaping our own identities. We are active agents.

In the covers of this book is my own pilgrimage in centering and integrating what has been helpful to me in my eleven years of pastoral counseling with black persons. Since this book represents my own journey, it can be of help to those who desire to become more the centering principle of their own lives. This book is not *the* response to modernity through pastoral counseling. Rather, it is *a response* I have found comfortable for me. Therefore, it will be helpful to those who are interested in developing pastoral styles that take into consideration their own dispositions as crucial in developing an approach to pastoral counseling. Effective pastoral counseling begins with the professional use of the self.

The book is divided into three major parts. The first part is an attempt to lay the theological and theoretical foundations for a value and spiritual orientation to pastoral counseling.

The first chapter will define the meaning of pastoral counseling in general, with specific reference to the black Christian experience. It will also provide a holistic perspective for understanding the human growth process, and the place of values and spiritual issues in this process. Chapters 2 and 3 will examine contemporary value and spiritual issues confronting families and pastoral counseling.

Part II is concerned with the role of pastoral care and counseling in facilitating the transmission of values, through the local church as a caring community, and through the family. There are two basic concepts in this discussion. One concept is structural, and the other reflects the functions and processes of the structure. These are the sociological concepts of mediating structure and nomos-building.

"Mediating structures are those institutions which stand between the individual in his private sphere and large institutions of the public sphere." One of the characteristics of modernity is the sweeping away of the "little aggregations" and leaving individuals to stand naked before large institutions. The result is that the individual is asked to create his or her own private sphere without any institutional support. Therefore, the task is to strengthen the mediating structures; namely the family, church, voluntary associations, neighborhood, and subcultures.[4] For life to have meaning, and for the individual to develop values and identity, mediating structures are essential. They support value formation.

One of the functions of mediating structures is to carry out the nomos-building task. This task focuses on the processes that assist the value formation tasks of mediating structures. Berger uses this concept in defining marriage as "a social arrangement that creates for the individual the sort of order in which he can experience his life as making sense." This nomos-building instrumentality helps to mediate the mores of society to the individuals within the family so that meaning results. Thus, developing significant relationships with others is crucial in helping people develop meaning in life. This observation led Berger to conclude that the stability of the world depends on the strength and continuity of significant relationships.[5]

This part delves into the role of pastoral counseling and care, the local church, and the family in mediating a meaningful world to people. In the world of social value flux, improving relationships with significant others is a must in order that wider social values and meaning be mediated to others. Thus, mediating structures and their nomos-building task give foundation, substance, and integrity to individual lives and give a feeling of belonging to an important community. How pastoral care and counseling can contribute to the maintenance of mediating structures and nomos-building is the subject of this part. Maintaining healthy relationships within the family and within the church makes a significant contribution to the establishment of personal values.

The third part of the book will explore how joint or couple marriage counseling as well as depth pastoral counseling can assist in the value transmission and formation process. Case studies will be used, and dream image theory from the work of Carl Jung is utilized to illustrate how dream images are an embodiment of values and of the transcendent, and how they can be used to reinforce the nomos-building process. Any expression of ministry, whether one-to-one or corporate, is a dimension of a larger Unity or a larger whole.

Many people were instrumental in the writing of this work. Immense gratitude once again to my beloved wife, Anne, whose loving and accepting way of life helped to nurture my ideas. Heartfelt thanks to my colleague Tom Pugh who encouraged my work concretely by administering financial resources set aside by the Theological Center. Deotis Roberts and Archie Smith, Jr., encouraged my work by affirming the value of what I was doing to their work as scholars. I am especially appreciative of Deotis Roberts' works, which make the development of the black family and the black church central in the liberation efforts of black people. I am also grateful for the critical review offered by

Manfred Hoffmann and Charles Gerkin at the beginning stages of this work. Thanks also to the *Journal of the Interdenominational Theological Center,* for granting me permission to use portions of two of my articles, "Pastoral Counseling and the Black Perspective," *Journal of the ITC* (Spring 1976), and "Pastoral Care and Support Systems," *Journal of the ITC* (Spring 1978). Finally, deep appreciation is extended to the able clerical and editorial assistance received from Barbara Holton, Sadye Gray, Willie Davis, Mrs. Willie Davis, and Judith Smith.

Edward P. Wimberly

PART I

Pastoral Counseling and Spiritual Values

This part of the book is an attempt to lay the theoretical and theological foundations for a value and spiritual orientation to pastoral counseling. The first chapter will define the meaning of pastoral counseling and a holistic understanding of the human growth process. The second chapter will examine the state of spirituality in pastoral counseling and its relevance to the black Christian community. The third chapter will examine the value issues confronting families in general and black families in particular in contemporary society and how the church can respond to these issues through ministry and pastoral counseling.

CHAPTER 1

Pastoral Counseling and Personality: Definitions

Pastoral counseling has an important role to play in contemporary black society and the church. Moreover, pastoral counseling, which involves the person and family, is not irrelevant to the black experience. Pastors will need increasing pastoral counseling skills in order to help liberate the minds, souls, and spirits of black people. Many people are discovering that, although changing society has great importance, it doesn't necessarily free people's minds. Often the slave mentality and damaged self-images persist and even resist liberation. Thus, liberation is more complex than first thought, and utopian social solutions to problems of oppression are limited and must be correlated with the tragic dimensions of sin that resist liberation. More and more, black pastors will need to address the forces within people that resist liberation as well as those inherent personal and spiritual resources that have the potential for setting people free.

PASTORAL COUNSELING

Pastoral counseling is the dimension of the liberation ministry of the church that is based upon a relationship between a pastor who has counseling skills and a person or

19

family who seeks out the pastor because they are in need of the pastor's counseling skills. This relationship has a definite structure and is based on certain agreed-upon goals. Moreover, there is an expectation on the part of the pastor and client[s] that the tradition of the church and its resources will be brought to bear, at some point in the counseling relationship, upon the needs of the person[s] seeking help. In this section the precise meaning of the concepts employed in this definition will be unravelled.

Pastoral counseling is a dimension of the liberation ministry of the church. Olin P. Moyd, in his book called *Redemption in Black Theology*, points out that liberation has three dimensions: (1) liberation from external oppression, (2) liberation from sin and guilt, and (3) liberation to share in community with others who are liberated.[1] Therefore liberation and redemption are a whole process and a unity, and emphasizing one dimension more than the other is a distortion of the essential unity of the gospel. Pastoral counseling, as defined here, takes this unity seriously and sees its task as being only one dimension of the liberation movement.[2] Pastoral counseling can never be *the* approach to ministry. However, other ministries are also only a part of a whole, just as pastoral counseling is part of a larger unity. All ministries together form an integrated unity known as liberation ministries.

Pastoral counseling, as one dimension of liberation ministry, seeks to accomplish the following goals: first, to help free people from those internal, interpersonal, and family shackles that prevent them from moving toward their full potential as children of God. Such liberation takes seriously the crippling social forces that influence people's lives, but it does not minimize the person's responsibility in how he or she chooses to respond to the social pressures. A great deal of the liberation effort in pastoral counseling seeks to develop responsibility, which is the ability to develop internal, interpersonal, spiritual, and moral resources in order to respond triumphantly to oppressive and disruptive forces. The second goal of pastoral counseling is to help people become free to respond to God's love in Jesus Christ through increasing their ability to grow in love toward God, self, and neighbor. Oppression from without is not the only oppressor. Sin, which is separation from God and being captive to destructive forces that prevent our growth, is also a crucial factor in crippling our ability to grow. Sin is the refusal to grow, preferring external and internal bondage because it is secure and keeps one's inner world safe. As the slave narratives indicate, some ex-slaves, like the children of Israel, preferred bondage to freedom.[3] Freedom and liberation require more personal responsibility than do slavery and bondage. While bondage did and does have its crippling and brutal dimensions, it also had its luring rewards for those who would rather have all their personal needs taken care of by others. Pastoral counseling seeks to free those who carry their slave mentality into freedom and who fail to take advantage of opportunities for growth that are placed before them daily. The goal is to help the person grow in love of his or her maker, in self-esteem and worth, and in love and service to others.

The third goal of pastoral counseling is to help release the power for growth and healing within individuals and families. On the personal level, power involves achieving the ability to actualize who one is as a unique person related to God, as well as to help others develop this capacity. This power is inherent in all people and families, but it often lies dormant. The pastoral counselor seeks to tap this latent resource, which will have the impact of bringing life and healing to people's lives.

Not only is pastoral counseling a part of the total liberation ministry of the church, but it is also a relationship. Pastoral counseling is a dynamic interactive process in which a caring connection is made between the pastoral counselor and the person[s] seeking help. The foundations of this relationship are the basic core relationship qualities of empathy, respect, genuineness, and concreteness. The source of these qualities of care is rooted in the Incarnation, by which God established a relationship of love and acceptance with humankind in the death, life, and resurrection of Jesus.

In pastoral counseling the task of the pastoral counselor is to create a relationship environment that facilitates the parishioner's or client's growth. The four dimensions mentioned above are core elements that must be present in the parishioner-client/pastoral counselor relationship if growth is to take place.[4] It is the counselor's responsibility to create the facilitative relationship by tuning in to the client's wavelength or seeing the world through the eyes of the client. This is empathy. The counselor must also respect the client's feelings and capacity to be responsible for him or herself. Respect is communicating concern and acceptance without rejecting the person's experiences and choices. The relationship is not exploitive, and is genuine in that he or she uses personal feelings facilitatively, not indiscriminately, to create a relationship. Finally, the relationship is facilitative when the pastoral counselor helps the client be specific about feelings, thoughts, and experiences.

Pastoral counseling is carried out by a pastor trained in counseling and psychotherapy. Pastoral counseling refers to a definite context in which counseling skills are applied. Pastoral counseling is done in a Christian context, and the pastoral counselor brings the training and skills learned in the counseling profession into the church and religious context. The Christian tradition has almost two thousand years of its own ministry style and caring, but the correlation of the Christian church context with counseling skills from the behavioral sciences makes pastoral counseling unique.

Pastoral counseling is not naive when it brings together two different traditions, the religious and the behavioral sciences. Pastoral counseling picks and chooses from the behavioral sciences only what is compatible with the mission of the church. Therefore, neither pastoral counseling nor the pastoral counselor is obligated to transport all the assumptions and goals of counseling into the pastoral context. The pastor is expected to develop his or her counseling acumen by drawing upon the training opportunities in the behavioral sciences and then correlating them with the mission or liberation goals of ministry. The ideal training opportunities are found in pastoral counseling training centers where the correlation of the two arenas is being carried out daily.

In pastoral counseling it is the general understanding that the person[s] in need will seek out the pastor. The pastoral relationship is sought and initiated because the person in need recognizes the need for help. This view of pastoral counseling is taken from the behavioral science one-to-one models and has come under attack from religious circles because it has limited all of the caring ministry to this model.

To understand the conflict between the one-to-one counseling model and the Christian context, it would be helpful to make a working rather than an absolute distinction between pastoral care and pastoral counseling. Pastoral care is one dimension of the liberating ministry of the church in which the total resources of the church are brought to bear upon a person and family in crisis. This definition reflects the church's traditional concern for seeking out the souls that need care. While the pastor and congregation take the initiative in pastoral care, pastoral counseling, following the behavioral science counseling model, is sought out by the person in need.

While there is a distinction between pastoral counseling and pastoral care, pastoral counseling is a dimension or extension of pastoral care, focusing on issues the pastor and counselee can agree on by open contract. In pastoral care the pastor or congregation takes the initiative because they recognize the need; however, in responding to that need, other needs may emerge that are recognized not only by the pastor but also by the parishioner. In this case, pastoral counseling takes place when a contract—a structure that contains the agreed-upon goals for the counseling relationship, including time, meeting place, and counselee commitment to the process—is made as a result of pastoral initiative. Therefore, pastoral counseling can grow out of pastoral care; it is not just confined to the parishioner's initiative. Given this conclusion, it is very difficult to make hard and fast distinctions between pastoral care and pastoral counseling. However, pastoral counseling does have an important place in pastoral care and in the church.

The expectations of both the pastor and the counselee play an important role in pastoral counseling. While the expectations of the counselee with regard to religious and spiritual issues are often vague and obscure, they are very much present. In the black context, they are often unrealistic expectations about the ability of the pastor to bring immediate relief or solutions to problems. Some counselees express their religious needs by expecting to be taken care of and protected by the pastor, which reflects the counselee's general expectations about religion. Some come with a more mature expectation to work through value and moral issues. Others come for help in accepting, understanding, and interpreting spiritual experiences and needs that make them feel unusual. Then there are those whose spiritual concerns emerge after many months, when emotional problems and anxiety are under control enough to let the spiritual self and its concerns emerge. Underlying all these concerns is the counselee's desire to make sense out of what is taking place inside and outside himself or herself. Here the spiritual and emotional problems are a search for meaning.

Not only does the counselee have certain expectations, but the pastoral counselor also has expectations. More and more pastoral counselors are taking their religious identity and context seriously and are waiting for opportunities to raise religious and spiritual issues with the client. One may hope that, in their training, pastoral counselors have been made aware of how often emotional problems of living are entangled in people's spiritual and ultimate concerns. When the timing is right, the pastoral counselor can gently urge the client to explore deeper spiritual concerns in the counseling relationship.

One additional word needs to be said about the methods of analogy used in this book. The method of analogy employed here is a borrowing procedure based upon substantive commitments. Substantive commitments are the loyalties held in the borrowing process.[5] Here the commitment is to the liberation mission of the church. Such borrowing seems arbitrary and capricious, particularly when the assumptions and frames of references differ from discipline to discipline. However, the method of analogy is not as arbitrary as it appears at first glance. The assumption implicit in my borrowing is that different disciplines often converge at many points, and one of these points is the theory of growth implied in them. Some interdisciplinary thinkers have gone as far as to say that the dimensions of growth—principles of wholeness, differentiation, and dynamic interaction—are common conceptual components of many of the behavioral sciences.[6] Recognizing that different disciplines have divergent assumptions and frames of reference is crucial, but this recognition does not preclude the use of borrowing by means of analogy. One is able to choose from other disciplines that which is analogous and corresponding to one's substantive loyalty. The integrity of all disciplines is maintained as long as one does not try to reduce the other disciplines to the substantive norm.

This book borrows many concepts from other disciplines on the basis of correspondence and convergence. Notable among these disciplines are sociology, systems theory, psychoanalytic theory, and theology and ministry.

PASTORAL COUNSELING AND THE BLACK PERSPECTIVE[7]

The unique emphasis in black pastoral care is derived from a perspective that has been shaped by the existential, cultural, and historical conditions peculiar to black people. This perspective reflects the cultural heritage of black people, their history as a people in a land of injustice, racism, and segregation, and their struggle as Christian people to make sense out of their existence in a hostile environment.

What, then, is this distinct emphasis that makes a black perspective in pastoral care and counseling unique? It is the corporate nature of pastoral care and counseling in the black church. Of course, there are white churches in Protestantism that have had a corporate emphasis in pastoral care and counseling, but the emphasis in white Protestantism has almost been exclusively individualistic, not corporate. It must also be added that many of the white Protestant seminaries are attempting now to bring the corporate emphasis into pastoral care, because the biblical emphasis is upon the corporate dimensions of human growth. It is also important to acknowledge that the history of American psychiatry shows a pendulum swing between the individual and corporate approaches in the 19th century.[8] However, the emphasis upon the individual and his or her self-sufficiency has been the dominant theme for most Americans, including the psychological and religious communities. On the other hand, the corporate emphasis among black Protestants has remained constant in their behavior, if not in attitude, due to the nature of black society and its cultural heritage from Africa.

The corporate nature of pastoral care and counseling in black Protestantism has its roots not only in African soil and racial discrimination in this country, but it also has them in the biblical conception of the nature of humanity and God's attempt to bring salvation. However, there is no attempt here to give a systematic explanation of the biblical contribution to pastoral care and counseling. The goal here is to establish the corporate function of pastoral care in the black church and, second, to discuss pastoral counseling in the light of recent research in the black community.

CORPORATENESS IN PASTORAL CARE

The nature of pastoral care and counseling in the black church is corporate for several reasons. The term *corporate* means that the care of the individual is the function of the whole community, rather than the function of the pastor or any other specially designated person who possesses specialized skills. The two outstanding influences that have historically contributed to the corporate nature of pastoral care are segregation and unconscious African survivals.

Segregation, which is the direct result of a rational attempt to justify slavery based upon the innate inferiority of black people, excluded the black person from full participation in the total life of the community. The black person was systematically excluded from normal access to avenues that could lead to fulfillment of his or her full potential as a whole person. The result of this exclusion was that the black church had to fulfill many of the political, social, educational, recreational, economic, and social needs of the black person. This was also true for the medical and mental health needs of the black person. Often it was the black church that took care of the needs of the neglected sick and mentally ill, because the hospitals and mental institutions were segregated. These persons were cared for by a caring community, because they could not be isolated from the community in the way that the white sick and mentally ill were.

The second influence that contributed to the corporate nature of black pastoral care was the unconscious survivals called Africanisms. These are African social patterns that persisted in Afro-American behavior. Indeed, there are many African survivals present in the life of the black community today. Many of them are the result of the transmission of social customs by fictive (nonblood) relationships established when unrelated slaves had been forced to work and live together. Many Africanisms were results of a sociohistorical past transmitted hereditarily through what Carl Jung calls the collective unconscious. Melville Herskovits, a noted American anthropologist, has spent his career developing the theory of the survival of Africanisms while doing comparative research.[9] The Africanisms for prime consideration here are the African philosophical concept of unity with nature, and the ritualistic, symbolic ceremonies that support the person in life crises.

The Africans believe that humanity exists in harmony with nature.[10] In this context people are not the manipulators or the controllers of the forces of nature, but humanity is to cooperate with nature.[11] The result of this philosophy is that the African sees the self and the community as integral parts of nature, and each influences the other. Thus, a person recognizes that his or her identity is the result of the interaction with nature and the environment.

To the African, not only is one's identity based upon the interaction with the physical environment, but it is also developed in relationship to the community. Mbiti points out that a child must be born, named, initiated, married—which are all functions of the community—before he or she can be thought of as a complete person.[12]

The implication of the concept of unity with nature and with the community is obvious for pastoral care. The collective unconscious of black people lends itself to the corporate concept. The corporate concept emerges from the African emphasis on unity with nature and forms the basis for an open systems approach to black pastoral care and counseling. It also forms a ground for building a personality theory that reflects the growth of the person in relationship to, and in interaction with, the community.

Another important factor in African religion that is of interest is the corporate nature of the symbolic, ritualistic ceremonies through which the African adjusted and coped with life crises in the past, and that survives in some of Africa today. Through the ceremonies surrounding birth, child rearing, initiation at adolescence, harvesting time, and death, the African found himself or herself in an ethos of ideological and emotional supports that helped him or her to overcome the crises of life. The same kind of support surrounding the life crises of black people, which became part of the black church, is an inheritance from the collective unconscious and the fictive relationships of non-blood kin who recreated what they remembered from their homeland. This support system is evidenced in the way the black church has been of real value in helping the black person deal with the problems associated with racism and injustice. Along with an ideological support system based upon the experience of black people with God and Jesus Christ—a support system reflected in the Negro spiritual—the African past has helped the black person and his community deal with the crises of life.

PASTORAL COUNSELING AND THE BLACK PERSON

From the preceding section one would perhaps conclude that pastoral counseling, a specialized area of pastoral care focusing on the needs of persons as individuals, is irrelevant to the work of the pastor in the black church or to the black pastoral counseling specialist. But it is conceivable that, along with the corporate dimensions and methods of black pastoral care, pastoral counseling can be used to help black people in need. In fact, there has been increasing evidence supporting the need for more training of black pastors in the specialty of pastoral counseling.

One source of the evidence of this need is the study done by my colleagues Thomas Pugh and Emily Mudd. Their study is on the attitudes of black women and men toward using community services.[13] Many of the respondents turned to families, kinfolk, and friends during marital difficulty, but they indicated that they would seek out professional help if it were available.

Another source of evidence is the study done on the black middle class in Philadelphia.[14] It reported a high degree of the use of medical caretakers who had sophisticated knowledge of emotional difficulty. With the availability of pastoral counselors with skills and training, people who are growing in their awareness of psychological services could use the pastoral counselor.

The evidence is not just limited to the black middle class. Perhaps the most convincing evidence of the viability of pastoral counseling in the black community comes from a study by Barbara Lerner called *Therapy in the Ghetto*. Her basic conclusion is that individual psychotherapy, under appropriate conditions, is an effective method of helping not only the traditional middle-class, highly verbal, intellectual client, but it also is of value to the so-called "non-classical untreatable" clients, such as the poor, the black, and the severely emotionally disturbed. These "untreatables" were thought to be poor risks in traditional therapeutic circles. The treatables were thought to be the young and attractive who possessed a high degree of ego-strength and who were well-educated members of the upper class.

Lerner found that measurable results of the treatment of non-treatable clients, when compared to the same changes in the traditional clients, have been achieved in less than thirty hours of treatment, or less than nine weeks.[15] It was found that 10-25 sessions were the normal length time for improvement in the presenting problem. Such facts warrant the consideration of psychotherapy in the black local church because of the short time involved in treatment. The pastor does not have a great deal of time to devote to counseling without neglecting other duties. The pastoral counseling specialist can take real encouragement from this study.

DEPTH PASTORAL COUNSELING IN THE BLACK EXPERIENCE

Depth pastoral counseling is not irrelevant to the needs of people in the black community. This is not only based upon the conclusions of Barbara Lerner, but it is also based upon my understanding of the unconscious psychic life revealed in the slave and ex-slave conversion experiences, Negro spirituals, and black dream folklore.[16] The inner life of black people is rich with imagery, and my own counseling practice has revealed that many of my black clients have a great deal of sophistication concerning the meaning and implications of dreams for everyday life. Any counseling methods that explore the dimensions of the unconscious, which are made manifest in dreams and symbolic images, have relevance to black people. Thus depth pastoral counseling, which is the plumbing of the depths of the unconscious resources for personality growth, has practical significance for the liberation ministry of the black church.

The richness of the inner psychic life of many black people can be seen in the conversion experiences of slaves and ex-slaves. Through the visions that precipitated the conversion, the resources of the spiritual world were made available to the inner psychic life through imagery. These images provided unmistakable clues to the great riddles and problems that the individual faced on the personal level, and the person experiencing the spiritual dimension drew upon these images to give guidance to his other life.

There is also a corporate dimension to these experiences of rich imagery. Worship and congregational praying often provided a warm, accepting atmosphere that facilitated openness to the spiritual world. This was true of the mourning bench tradition during revivals where caring people prayed and sang with seeking people until they had an encounter with the divine.[17] This experience of the loving care of others and of an encounter with God was often accompanied by powerful images that the congregation waited anxiously to hear about from the experiencer. Hearing the seeker's testimony strengthened the church's faith and reinforced the experiencer's faith.

Dreams were also part of the corporate context in the black community. However, the context was one of folklore where the community interpretive system had specific meanings for different images. Many of the interpretations had to do with birth and death. If someone dreamed of fish, it was an omen of a new addition to the family, according to my father's small-town community in central Florida.

Although the manifestation of people's inner psychic life originally had a community context, my own use of dreams in depth pastoral counseling with black persons has convinced me of the relevance of this form of pastoral counseling to black people. Dream interpretation, which draws upon the social context and meanings from the person's own life, is very helpful to the black client. Moreover, some of the suggestions offered in Jungian psychology have assisted in bringing out the contextual meaning of dreams and their implications for the dreamer in my pastoral counseling. The dreams of clients often have spiritual significance revealing deep stirrings in the soul, and attention to the dreams has helped make spiritual concerns part of the counseling.

PASTORAL COUNSELING AND VALUES

Values indicate what is important and significant to people, and they are crucial to pastoral care and counseling. Historically, pastoral care in the black church was a mediator of the symbolic world-view that communicated to the black person the following values: (1) the inherent worthiness of each person as unique, (2) the inner potential for growth and development in relationship to God and others, (3) the primacy of caring relationships and supportive relationships in community, and (4) the power of God working through the community as well as the unconscious to build up the lives of the community and its people. These values and the meaning that they brought to people's lives were not only part of a symbolic world-view, they were also embodied in people and in concrete relationships. People were carriers of these values, as well as vehicles for the manifestation of the Source of these values, and when people came into contact with each other, these values were shared. Moreover, the Source of these values was continually worshiped, and the environment of the worship helped to strengthen the values. As individuals encountered each other and worshiped together, they were reminded of their common life and of their significance as worthwhile people.

Just as the values and their Source were available to those in an encounter with the community of carers, these same resources are available through pastoral care and counseling as relationship. Thus, an encounter with a pastoral counselor, who is rooted in a caring community that has its source in God, communicates God's concern for the counselee, and the love of the community.

Because pastoral counseling is a part of a community that has divine and value resources, the pastoral counselor must never be cut off from the community of believers. The task of the pastoral counselor is to keep rooted in the Source as well as the caring community so that the values can be mediated to others. Being cut off from the community itself is less likely to happen, because pastoral care, by its very definition, makes this an impossibility.

Being part of the caring community and remaining in constant contact with the Source of value makes pastoral counseling a real possibility in the black church. Without this context, any form of counseling that utilizes the one-to-one model is suspect. However, in the caring community context this model is very appropriate in the black church.

THE NATURE OF PERSONALITY

Every theory of pastoral counseling has an implicit or explicit understanding of how people grow. This understanding includes ideas about the worth of persons, the factors that contribute to the growth of persons, and the nature of personality itself. This section will outline the personality theory undergirding the theory of pastoral counseling developed in the previous sections. The basic assumption underpinning this section is that the purpose of pastoral counseling is to help release the potential for self-actualization and for growth.

Personality can be defined as a system composed of dynamic, interacting, and interdependent parts that has continuity in time and determines one's thoughts, actions, and feelings.[18] The personality is not a closed system, but an open system that grows in interaction with the wider systems in which the person participates. The personality has an internal governing agent, sometimes called the *ego,* which keeps the organism functioning in continuity in spite of the constant feedback from external and internal systems.

The personality system is made up of a variety of subsystems. These subsystems are: (1) physiological, (2) intrapsychic, (3) interpersonal, and (4) spiritual. The physiological subsystem is the physical components of the body—the cardiovascular, respiratory, nervous, digestive, and reproductive subsystems. The intrapsychic system is composed of what Carl Jung calls the conscious, personal unconscious, and collective unconscious dimensions. The interpersonal system is a sense of self acquired in the performance of social roles. The spiritual system is the dimension of the personality system that relates one to the depth of reality, the sources of meaning, and to the cosmos and God. All four of these subsystems interact with each other and with the environment. This dynamic interaction forms an important mix, which in turn influences one's thoughts, feelings, and actions.

The intrapsychic subsystem needs to be clarified in further detail. The conscious dimension of this subsystem is composed of that material (thoughts, feelings, memories) of which one is aware. This dimension of the system is usually governed by the ego, whose task is to maintain a steady state within the total personality system. The ego's task is to regulate the input received from the physiological, inter-personal, and spiritual subsystems.

While the conscious contains the material of which one is aware, the personal unconscious contains that material of which one is unaware. This material includes forgotten instinctual impulses associated with the physiological subsystem that are threatening to the conscious life of the person. The personal unconscious also includes a dimension Freud calls the *super-ego*. This is the internalized moral system that has been developed as a result of interaction with society and social roles. Often this dimension must remain outside conscious awareness because it frequently comes into conflict with the physiological requirements of the body.

The collective unconscious, in Jungian psychology, goes far beyond the personal unconscious in that it contains more than threatening memories, thoughts, and feelings. It also contains one's social, racial, historical, and ontological past. Human beings have access to resources belonging to another time, place, and reality through the collective unconscious. Through dreams, visions, and images, this resource and reservoir can be made available to persons.

The collective unconscious is often the source or reservoir of spiritual experiences. While we classify the spiritual subsystem separately from the intrapsychic subsystem, the collective unconscious concept provides the psychological background for understanding the spiritual dimension. Spiritual resources, like historical and racial resources, are often made available through images that appear through the collective unconscious.

The subsystems of the personality are not mutually exclusive or separate. Rather, they overlap and interpenetrate. It is not so easy to differentiate them from the other subsystems. Therefore, the subsystems are essentially related to each other.

Goal Direction

Crucial to the understanding of personality is the concept of striving, which refers to the attempt by each system to realize itself or to become complete. Each system and subsystem within the personality, the family, community, and culture functions in a way based upon the growth or development model, and in this model, growth is teleological, or purposive and goal-directed. Within the personality each system or subsystem has enough drive, push, or energy to propel it toward its potentiality. Thus, in Jungian language, there is a force within the personality and within each of its subsystems that pushes for and toward creativity.

Conflict exists in this fulfillment or growth model of personality when each system has to work in concert with the others in order to develop the whole organism to completeness. For example, the physiological system pushes the person toward physical development and maturation. Yet this may conflict with the moral subsystem within the personality that has been internalized as the result of interaction with societal norms. Moreover, there may be a conflict when internalized societal bias against spirituality, which has developed as the personality interacted with wider society, clashes with the emerging spiritual concerns of the person. Thus, fulfillment can lead to conflict.

If conflict of this nature does emerge, it is the function of the ego, the conscious dimension of the personality, to keep the personality in a steady state in order to assure the continuity of the whole organism. Therefore, the striving of each system and subsystem within the personality to realize itself must be orchestrated into a symphonic whole by the ego.

The Self and the Ego[19]

The ego has been defined as the governing agent of the personality that keeps the organism from dissolving when all the systems are in interaction within the personality, and as these internal factors interact with wider society. As such, the ego cannot be the center of the personality in that it cannot characterize precisely all that emerges from the interaction of the various subsystems within the personality. In this context the *self* is the dimension of personal awareness that emerges as the result of, or output of, the personality functioning as a system. That is, the self is the sense of "I" that results from the personality system's functioning. The "I" emerges as one moves from a stage in which one is identified with and is undifferentiated from the family, to a stage where a differentiated state exists and one is aware of oneself as a separate and autonomous entity. A sense of "I" or "me" is crucial because this is the goal of the self-actualization process. The individual grows in the developmental cycle from an undifferentiated symbiotic relationship with the family toward an autonomous exis-tence, and when persons move toward greater degrees of autonomy, the sense of "I" or "me" becomes more intact.

To avoid the pejorative understanding of the sense of "I," it is important to talk about the concept of centering. The "I" or "me" referred to here has nothing to do with an idolatrous or narcissistic "me" that withdraws from social participation, intimacy, and communion, into a selfism characterized by self-worship and the feeling that one is totally sufficient unto oneself. Rather, the "I" refers more to finding a sense of self rooted in meaning or in what Erik Erikson calls ego-integrity.[20] A real sense of self requires that a person be a participant and centered in something that transcends him or her and the family, and that helps the person make sense out of life. This process of finding the transcendent base to personality that gives meaning to life is called *centering*. Therefore, while the sense of "I" means differentiation into a sense of self, it also means a radical participation in something beyond the self. Thus the roots for autonomy, self actualization, and individualization are found in participating in something that transcends the self and the family. In a real way, the ability to become an "I" or a "me" separate from others requires, paradoxically, a giving up of the self to a higher reality.

Since the centering of the self is something that transcends self, it is not, then, solely the product of the system's functioning. The self is contextual—influenced by interaction with the variety of systems that make up the individual. Yet it is not a passive entity. Rather, it is an active participant in its own creation and, because of this, it can transcend the processes that influence it. This ability to transcend is rooted in the centering and, as a result of centering, the person can be influenced while transcending the influence.

Because of the centering ability of the self, one of its characteristics is that it is self-reflective. That is, the self has the ability to dialogue with itself and make the self an object of itself.[21] For example, the self can dialogue with itself, have conceptions about itself, and act toward itself. As such, the self can transcend itself and stand outside itself. This is the true meaning of self-transcendence.

When the self has the ability to stand outside itself, it has the potential to stand toward God. True centering takes place when the self stands outside itself, its systems' interaction, and its family, and stands in God. To stand in God is to stand in the ultimate source of meaning for the self. And this enriches the whole life of the person. More precisely, it gives the person wholeness.

The Soul

The foundation of the self's ability to be centered and stand in God is the soul. The soul can be defined as the dimension of the self through which God and individuals are related. Here the soul is the conveyor of one's primal identity or essential identity with God. The soul is the vehicle through which one's true identity with God is established, and through which God reconciles the self to Him, the ultimate Source of meaning.[22]

When the person stands in the ultimate Source of meaning, the person has a resource to draw upon for making sense out of life. The resources are apprehended through intuition at the times of crises and are manifested through internal realities of the person as well as through existing social values. Thus, ultimate values that can enhance growth are an ever present resource to be drawn upon.

CONCLUSION

The corporate nature of personality must be taken seriously by pastoral counseling. When this is done, pastoral counseling will become corporate pastoral counseling seeking to help people become self-actualized, individuated people centered in God and ultimate meaning. Our task as pastoral counselors is to facilitate a systematic growth process through which people can become whole.

CHAPTER 2

The Recovery of the Soul in Pastoral Counseling: Moral and Spiritual Implications

INTRODUCTION

Early in my counseling experience I spent several years working with a young lady whose self-image was severely damaged as a result of a separation from her husband. Her husband had left her for another woman, and this unfortunate occurrence precipitated a series of acts that led to an acute depression. One result was that she became engaged in a casual sexual relationship. This relationship was only initiated to show her husband that she could indeed live without him, that other men were interested in her, and that she wasn't hurt by his desertion. Her behavior was designed to convince her husband that she was all right and not suffering any pain. However, she was suffering a great deal of pain in spite of her external appearance, and to make matters worse, she had gotten pregnant in the casual relationship. This led to an abortion, which only added more losses to the ones she had already sustained.

I learned a very important lesson from working with this woman. As I began to respond to her immediate emotional problems with loss and abandonment, other depth dimensions of her personality began to emerge, such as the pain she had experienced with both parents. Her mother and father were both killed in a car accident and left her and eight other brothers and sisters to be raised by an older sister who was in her late teens. Because of the severe losses suffered, I felt that the prognosis for her recovery from the losses was dreary. In fact, I felt that she was too victimized by life's cruelty and the only help I thought I could give was to provide sustaining counseling that would prevent any further deterioration of her present emotional state. I felt that growth in personality dimensions was remote, if not non-existent; therefore, we contracted for supportive counseling.

As we moved forward in the counseling contract, it soon became apparent that many possibilities for growth existed, and I had suffered from the phenomenon called premature closure. I learned that it is always important to avoid circumscribing the human growth potential. To my surprise and delight, I discovered that there existed a great potential for growth within my client. As a result, the contract was changed from supportive counseling to long-term counseling focusing on her self-image problems and ways she could improve her feelings about herself.

After several years of counseling with this client, I learned another important lesson about the human personality. I had thought that moral and spiritual issues would not be significant in counseling; however, as she gained more confidence in herself and discovered more positive dimensions of her personality, moral and spiritual issues began to dominate the sessions. She began to raise questions concerning her mission and purpose in life. She began to talk about her real feelings about her abortion and came to the point of confessing that she felt she had taken the life of an unborn person and truly felt the need to be forgiven.

In this specific case I learned that people cannot be confined to neat categories of emotional and psychological responses. People are more than complexes, drives, anxieties, or neuroses. We have religious, spiritual, and moral concerns, and these concerns are often hidden. Moreover, these concepts emerge and become part of the counseling sessions in which we participate as counselors. Indeed, people are complex wholes, and this realization has made me more sensitive to spiritual and religious issues that emerge in the counseling relationship.

Persons are indeed dynamic and complex, and pastoral counselors need to develop what Charles Gerkin calls a breadth of perspective[1] when we are assessing someone's personality resources. More precisely, we need to examine each person from a variety of perspectives in order to produce insights into the depth, width, and height of the total personality, as far as this is possible. In addition to this, we need to broaden our therapeutic arsenal so that it complements the understanding of persons as whole beings. We have far too long been encapsulated by a scientific and technological way of looking at persons, so much so that we have almost unconsciously limited and restricted our understanding of the complexity of human beings.

More than having just a breadth of perspective, we also need a breadth of vision that includes theological and spiritual dimensions and understandings of human beings. Such a perspective would help to bring pastoral counseling closer to its Christian heritage. We need to broaden our understanding of the human personality, particularly the spiritual and moral aspects and their implications for pastoral counseling.

The discussion in this chapter is divided into four areas. The first focuses on the importance of the soul dimension in the black experience. The second concerns the present state of pastoral counseling and its relationship to spirituality; the third concerns the modern person's need for meaning and the inability of current symbols to provide that meaning; and the fourth concerns how pastoral counseling and guidance might be one of many solutions to contemporary humanity's pursuit of meaning.

THE SOUL DIMENSIONS OF BLACK CHRISTIAN EXPERIENCE

There are five basic themes that have emerged from black Christian experience that give uniqueness to that experience.

These dimensions are (1) the corporate understanding of the human personality, (2) the protest theme, (3) the emphasis on support systems, (4) a belief in an active God of history working in behalf of the poor and oppressed, and (5) a belief in the soul as closely akin to God. The first four themes were treated in detail in my doctoral dissertation,[2] and the fifth theme has emerged as a result of studying slave conversion experiences.[3] Ample examination has already been given to the first four themes in the dissertation and in *Pastoral Care in the Black Church*, but little attention has been given to a black Christian belief in the soul. Therefore, some attention will be given to this belief in this section. The basic assumption underlying these five dimensions of the black Christian experience is that all these aspects are a unity that is part of a larger unity, and pastoral care and counseling cannot ignore the essential unity of all reality.

In the mind of the slave and ex-slave, as well as in the African past (as far as the writer can interpret), the physical and spiritual worlds were mutually influential and interpenetrating, rather than separate entities, as in Platonic and other Greek thought. Therefore, there was a this-worldly and an other-worldly orientation, but they were not mutually exclusive with fixed boundaries. The spiritual world and the physical world interacted continually, and the vehicle for this continual feedback was the soul. The soul, which was closely akin to God, was not confined to the body and material realm, but was mobile and often left at night while the sleeper slept.[4] In fact, the soul often frequented the spiritual realm, replenishing the psyche and the personality while the person was resting. In this sense, the soul and its work took place on the unconscious level.

Pastoral counseling in a black context must take very seriously the unity of all experience and not neglect the spiritual yearnings of the soul. In unity the soul cannot be viewed as separate from other dimensions, except for the purposes of academic analysis.

Throughout this work the soul will be considered a purposive entity that pushes the person toward self-transcendence and toward unity with the ultimate source of the soul's activity. This understanding of the soul grows out of, and is consistent with, the black Christian understanding of the soul.

In the next sections the difficulty that the Euro-American model of pastoral counseling has with the concept of the soul will be explored, and suggestions for the use of the soul perspective for pastoral counseling, and for counseling with black Christians in particular, will be examined.

THE DILEMMA OF PASTORAL COUNSELING

Carl Jung pointed out that three-fourths of the persons coming to him for therapy after or during middle age came, not because of emotional issues alone, but because of spiritual or religious issues.[5] These issues concerned the person's place in the universe and problems of ultimate meaning. While the first half of one's life is directly related to meeting the expectations of society, the last half of life needs to have a foundation that is more spiritual and inward. This same observation is made in Erik Erikson's work, especially when he talks about the last stage of maturational development, or the stage of ego-integration or despair.[6] Erich Fromm also supports this notion of a spiritual need in the middle-aged person, but he indicates that psychoanalysis and psychotherapy are not equipped to handle this spiritual and religious need. I will analyze Fromm's observations concerning the art of therapy, because similar comments can be made about pastoral counseling.

According to Fromm, psychoanalysis is not equipped to deal with spiritual and religious concerns because it has abandoned its historical relationship with the psychology and philosophy of the past. Historically, psychology and philosophy were related, and their focus was on the soul, which, he postulates, has to do with the higher powers of the human personality, such as love, reason, conscience, and values. This discontinuity between the past and the present came as a result of developments in the academic world of psychology, according to Fromm. He feels that academic psychology has tried to imitate the natural sciences and its experimental methodologies. In this scientific orientation, dimensions such as values, conscience, and knowledge of good and evil were pushed aside and relegated to philosophy, and declared insignificant for psychology. Fromm concludes that "psychology thus became a science lacking its main subject matter, the soul."[7] Therefore, psychotherapy's primary preoccupation became "mechanisms, reaction formations, and instincts," and not the most significant human soul qualities.

Fromm's analysis can also be applied to pastoral counseling. A distinction must first be made, however, between what Fromm understood to be the soul and how I am using the soul in this presentation. Fromm's concept of soul is that of a humanistic soul having an ontological base in the structure of reality; yet this base has no specific theological referent. It confines itself to philosophical parameters and relates to the universal values of truth, love, and responsibility. Here I want to employ Fromm's philosophical notion of the soul, as well as a black Christian perspective that regards the soul as the aspect of the person that enables the person to have direct access to the ultimate source of truth, values, creativity, and love; namely, God. The soul, as understood here, has humanistic as well as transcendent-divine dimensions, and it is the latter understanding that has given our profession of pastoral counseling some difficulty.

Many pastoral counselors have abandoned the soul, particularly in the theological language symbols already employed here. While William Hulme has pointed out that God talk has a place in the new identity of pastoral counselors,[8] many of us are still guilty of scientific reductionism and the secularization of our pastoral perspectives and practices. That is, we are often prone to ignore promptings within our clients that behavioral science terminology is inadequate to designate. If we do recognize spiritual stirrings within clients, we are reluctant to attach transcendent labels to them for fear of the implications such identification might have for our own spiritual pilgrimage. Dealing with the transcendent dimension of spirituality is a threat to many pastoral counselors. Sometimes it is much easier to deal with personality growth toward wholeness and self-actualization than with the soul in relationship to the ultimate. I recognize that I may be overstating the case a little to make a point. Indeed, wholeness and self-actualization are a part of the larger processes I label spirituality. What I am really addressing is a scientific form of conceptualizing that dismisses a spiritual dimension of reality.

Gerald May has done some conceptualizing about the threat to pastoral counselors in the use of concepts of soul and spirituality. He is concerned that pastoral counselors may be frightened that spirituality may have very deep implications for their self-image that they are not ready to handle. He says:

> My experience has led me even further to believe in the deep threat that spirituality poses to one's image of one's self. And I am forced to think that this is still the primary motivation behind the reluctance of many pastoral counselors to discuss spiritual issues openly with clients.

He continues:

> It's hard enough when one's devoting one's self to work on psychological and interpersonal problems. But it becomes far more difficult when spiritual issues are confronted. Thus it remains true that the clergy, who are the recipients of such terribly heavy spiritual expectation, have the hardest time in confronting the raw energy of human spirituality in a counseling situation.[9]

Here Gerald May is referring to transference problems encountered in therapy, and these transference issues are doubly difficult to confront when accompanied by spiritual expectations. Yet relating to spiritual transference is crucial and has theological significance with special reference to the doctrine of idolatry. At the heart of the spiritual transference phenomenon is the placing of a limited human object at the center of one's life and expecting divine results from such a placement. Indeed, this is a very difficult form of transference to confront when the counselor is the object of expectation. Yet it becomes less of a threat to confront if the pastoral counselor permits himself or herself to develop his or her own spirituality and to explore in depth her or his own spiritual needs and expectations of others. It is important that we pastoral counselors embark upon our own spiritual journeys, so that we can become guides leading others where we have traveled. We need to tend to our own spiritual needs, so that when we encounter others less mature in the journey, we can help them find ways and sources to meet their deepest need. It is very difficult to help people go where we are reluctant to travel.

Perhaps we need to end our romance with scientific models of therapy long enough to develop a sensitivity to genuine and authentic religious and spiritual hungers that our clients confront in their lives. Moreover, we pastoral counselors must overcome our own fear of the fundamentalism and the magical religious orientations that have characterized many of our backgrounds and that prevent our relating to the client's spiritual need. More and more people will be seeking us out, searching for genuine religious solutions to emotional and spiritual problems. It remains to be seen whether we will be able to respond to these concerns.

Studies are appearing now that indicate that spiritual experiences, whether labeled religious, transcendent, or humanistic, are very much part of the experiences of Americans.[10] This has led Dr. Archie Smith, a black pastoral counselor and professor on the faculty of the Pacific School of Religion, to say that spirituality "is common to all living beings and exists as a relationship concept with other dimensions of the personality."[11] Such a generalized conclusion has profound implications for pastoral counselors, if we accept this statement as true or plausible. Our task, professionally and religiously, is to relate the whole person; and this pertains not only to the emotional issues, but also to issues related to spiritual and moral concerns. Even if the transcendent labels are unacceptable, we still must at least go as far as Erich Fromm has gone. There are, indeed, strivings within the human breast that push us far beyond social and psychological prescriptions, and we should try to be sensitive to them.

THE SOCIAL DILEMMA

The dilemma of pastoral counseling and psychotherapy has roots in wider society and in historical developments that extend beyond academic psychology. Exploration of our socio-historical context will lay the groundwork for outlining the task of pastoral counseling in the rest of this century and for many years to come. This analysis will lift up the central psychological and spiritual needs that people will manifest and that will be of paramount importance in the immediate future.

Ernest Becker, in *The Denial of Death,* makes a major critique of psychoanalysis, and his examination links the crisis of psychoanalysis with the crisis of society. He points out that the failure of psychoanalysis is that it has not taken into consideration that neurosis and psychosis are a cultural response to the collapse of cultural symbols.[12] Cultural symbols are the fundamental building blocks of universes of meanings. Adequate symbols are needed for people to develop a meaningful philosophy of life, to struggle with ultimate meaning, to link present values with past values, and to assist people in identity formation. Here *symbol* refers to forms that point to concrete values or meanings that give human behavior significance. The significance of symbols can be envisioned in Jung's understanding of the symbol (as summarized by Ira Progoff). "If a culture fails to maintain psychologically effective symbols, its individuals withdraw from social areas of life and turn into themselves in search of new meaning."[13]

There is a relationship between personality development and social symbols. Symbols are the result of social interaction and interpretive processes that are formed, sustained, and transformed to give the world meaning.[14]

Customs and traditions are often the custodians of symbols, and when these are changed substantially, there is a corresponding change in personality development. Symbols, as part of the tradition, help provide the context and avenues for discovery of new meaning, but when the established mechanism that provides the context and continuity for creative meaning is destroyed, personality development becomes more difficult. Personality growth requires a stable cultural value system, and when this system does not exist, the individual must find ingenious ways to create one. Without custom, tradition, and values, a personality loses its social continuity.

The loss of the soul-concept in pastoral counseling and psychoanalysis has to be viewed in the context of the collapse of cultural symbols. Sociologists like Peter Berger point out that the collapse of enduring symbols is the result of the impact of technological development upon society. The result has been secularism and privatism. These two concepts need some elaboration in detail.

Technological culture is characterized by rational, scientific symbols based upon experimentation, reason, observation, objectivity, and facts. In addition to scientific assumptions, technological symbols have replaced religious symbols in helping persons to find ways to derive meaning from the complexities of life, such as the problem of suffering and evil. In some quarters, experimental scientism has taken over the role of religion and has brought with it an expectation that death and suffering can be overcome by science. One negative result of this scientism is that many of the traditional ways for understanding the universe and our place in it have been undermined. Many religious symbols have been replaced as a result of the emergence of technology, and the transcendent dimension has been removed from cultural symbolic systems. This process of removing transcendent and religious symbols from the societal meaning system is called *secularization.*

When the sacred was removed from cultural symbolism, the soul, as that dimension that related people to God, became unimportant. In fact, many people tried to bury God once and for all. However, our need for a transcendent symbol system did not die. It was either denied or projected onto a newfound belief in the power of science and the human potential for unlimited achievement.

Accompanying secularism has been the denial of the spiritual dimension as well as the soul dimension. Peter Berger points out that the repression of the transcendent has been socially and culturally institutionalized to the point where any reference to the transcendent is censored, ignored, and abandoned.[15] According to Gerald May, technological symbols are characterized by a spiritual Victorianism, in which the spiritual and soul needs of persons have been repressed, much as the sexual need had been in the Victorian period of history which formed the background of Freud's psychology.[16]

In this environment of spiritual repression and secularity, a great deal of responsibility has been placed on individuals to create their own symbols and meaning. The need for values—to help give meaning to life and to help people find their place in the cosmos and to live in spite of suffering, pain, and death—has not disappeared. This need has been denied or projected to scientific symbols, and when this proved inadequate, individuals have turned to private and inward means to find meaning. This turning inward is called *privatism* by sociologists, and is characterized by a consumer attitude: one selects one's own value orientation from a variety of competing values.[17] This puts a lot of responsibility on the individual, a responsibility cultural symbols formerly had.

People today have discovered their own spiritual needs and the inability of a scientific world-view to meet these needs. This observation has been confirmed by people like Gerald May, Erich Fromm, Carl Jung, Peter Berger, and Ernest Becker. Gerald May points out that it is easy to understand the current emphasis on spirituality when there have been many years of repression. Ernest Becker says that the need for transcendent symbols, including concepts like the soul, only goes underground in a scientific culture; only to appear later as an energized need seeking insatiably for satisfying objects. Indeed, culture has failed, and so has pastoral counseling, in helping people meet their spiritual needs. As Archie Smith has stated, spirituality and the need for transcendent realities are common to all of us, and people are looking for adequate symbols to meet and express these needs. Symbols, which can be defined not only as creations of social interaction, but also as vehicles of meaning in the structure of reality, will become a major concern of pastoral counseling in the future.

The major need confronting all of us as pastoral counselors and pastors in the remainder of this century will be the need of individuals for a symbolic universe capable of helping them make sense of this universe characterized by suffering, injustice, and death. In the words of Ernest Becker, "We need the boldest creative myths, not only to urge men on but also and perhaps especially to help men see the reality of their condition."[18]

PASTORAL COUNSELING: TODAY AND TOMORROW

In the current climate of cultural value flux and the loss of enduring values, what is the role of pastoral counseling? The thesis of this section is that pastoral counseling has a crucial role to play in helping people develop value perspectives, as well as in helping them develop their spiritual lives.

The moral role of pastoral care as been highlighted by Don S. Browning in *The Moral Context of Pastoral Care,* which deals with the present socio-cultural situation. He examines the tremendous impact that modernism has had on our daily living, especially with regard to pluralism and competing values. He points out that the impact has been negative, and that the real need in today's society is to help people develop meaningful value systems that will inform all dimensions of life. He further believes that pastoral care and counseling have reflected the confusion of values that has existed at the wider cultural level; and because of this, it is not in a position to influence many people who are searching and reaching out for self-control and self-transcendence. He argues that pastoral care and counseling have abandoned moral guidance in a time when there needs to be clarification of normative values in people's lives. In response to this neglect of moral values in pastoral counseling, his solution is the reclamation by pastoral care of the socioethical context of Pharisaic Judaism. This tradition is characterized by practical moral rationality built on an interpretation and implementation of convenantal law. Thus, taking its lead from practical moral rationality, pastoral care should create a moral context for inquiry into moral questions that affect the lives of counselees. Browning's approach is not the imposition of Old Testament covenantal law on contemporary life; rather, it is the creation of an atmosphere within the church where people can actually develop the moral dimensions of their lives.

While Browning's thesis is fascinating and points to the moral task of pastoral care, it neglects the important roles that psychoanalytic models of pastoral counseling can play in the modern era. The real question is, What role does contemporary pastoral counseling play in the moral and spiritual quest of humanity? Browning's model attempts to respond to this question by introducing pastoral guidance. However, if we confine ourselves to his model alone, we might miss the tremendous resources inherent in the human personality for value formation, and the role that pastoral counseling has in tapping this moral and spiritual reservoir within all of us. While it has been pointed out that people will turn inward for meaning when cultural symbols fail, this is not all bad; in fact, it may point to a more fundamental process that originally gave rise to values.

This presentation takes a point of view similar to that of Erich Fromm. For him, the cure of souls involves the "optimal development of a person's individuality."[19] Foundational to Fromm's view of the cure of souls is his belief that there are immutable laws inherent in the human personality that are operative in all humans, regardless of culture, and these laws are part of the structure of reality. Therefore, as people achieve self-actualization, they will grow and mature in truth and integrity. In actualizing themselves, they are fulfilling a potential that already existed within themselves and within the structure of reality. Not only does one's integrity increase in self-actualization, one grows in one's ability to love and to take responsibility for oneself. Thus, to become self-actualized is to develop the moral and spiritual potential that is already inherent within oneself.

In Fromm's way of thinking, the current moral and spiritual dilemma can be solved by turning inward. However, this turning inward must not be misunderstood as narcissistic disengagement and withdrawal from participation in social reality and relationships. Rather, it is an inward movement to find truth, justice, love, and an object of devotion, all of which have their roots in the unconscious.[20] When one turns inward, one encounters not only one's own socialized history, memories, and forgotten experiences, but also one's inherent potentialities that have an objective reality beyond the person. Thus, the unconscious is a reservoir of the highest and best that is available to humankind.

In order to help clarify Fromm's position on the inward journey and to make his argument a little more convincing, I will refer to the works of Carl Jung. In fact, Fromm draws upon Jung's understanding of the collective unconscious for his own definition of the unconscious. For Jung, the collective unconscious goes far beyond Freud's notion of the unconscious as a reservoir of instincts pushing for immediate gratification. The collective unconscious is, rather, a reservoir of the social, racial, psychological, and ontological history of humankind. It contains moral and spiritual solutions to problems, solutions humankind has developed and used since time began. The unconscious solutions address ultimate theological issues such as good, evil, suffering, injustice, and the paradoxes and contradictions of life. More than this, the collective unconscious is a vehicle through which people can find ways to be united with the cosmos and the ground of being. To turn inward, then, is to encounter more than one's own limited self.

Crucial to the discussion here, is the notion that societal values that were once alive and thriving become part of an unconscious reservoir, which becomes an everlasting present resource. Values have continuity and are active at the depths of the human psyche.[21] They exist whether civilizations rise or wane. 'They persist as part of the collective unconscious, waiting to be discovered, reexamined, and reappropriated within the individual's life.

Jung and Fromm's thinking, when added to the black Christian understanding of the soul, has implications for pastoral counseling. The first implication is that pastoral counseling can develop broader perspectives for dealing with moral and spiritual issues. In fact, from this perspective, every counseling hour has the potential for dealing with moral and spiritual issues. This conclusion is based upon an understanding of people as wholes, whose emotional, spiritual, and moral dimensions are difficult to separate. Yet the implicit spiritual issues need to be made more explicit in a society whose traditional conveyers of values are breaking up. In the past, traditional vehicles of values had an unquestioned significance underlying them, and did not need to be made explicit by the individual to have their impact.[22] However, the implicit models of conduct and interpretive schemes working in culture to help guide persons are no longer as binding as they once were; therefore, externalization, or making explicit the values that emerge from the unconscious realm, is very important today. The moral guidance from within, based on insight from the unconscious, needs to become more conscious and rational to replace the void left by tradition.

The second implication of this thinking is that pastoral guidance and spiritual counseling and direction take on a new meaning. Throughout its history, pastoral care has attempted to help people make confident choices between alternative courses of action, and this had been done in two chracteristic ways; through inductive and educative guidance.[23] According to Clebsch and Jaekle, inductive guidance sought to help people make choices based upon a priority set of principles, while educative guiding focused on helping decision-making by drawing upon hidden values in the person. The soul perspective here has helped us recognize that inductive and educative guidance are not as distinct as their definitions imply. Moving inward to a universal reservoir of value exposes the person to values that were at one point external to the person. Values—whether internal or external—are part of a larger unity. Therefore moving inward, which is necessitated by the times we live in, has an inductive dimension to it. The pastoral guide helps the person to base a decision on inherent values within rather than basing it on an external value system. The underlying assumption is that value systems, whether internal or external, have the same source.

Spiritual counseling, like moral guidance, is gaining prominence in our culture today. The same issue exists between spiritual guidance and direction as exists between inductive and educative guidance. According to Gerald May, a spiritual counselor helps people talk about, explore, and clarify their spiritual needs and experiences.[24] On the other hand, the spiritual director, like the inductive spiritual guide, helps people develop methods of responding to their spiritual needs by teaching specific methods of praying and of deriving greater spiritual meaning by drawing upon tradition. Here again, the distinction between the spiritual counselor and the spiritual director is hard to make when one recognizes that the same resources available in tradition and within the depths of the person have the same source, which is a universal reservoir having an independent existence, apart from the person and the tradition that conveys it. Pastoral counselors do not have to feel that they are abandoning the moral and value dimensions of persons' lives when they practice their art. Rather, they need to recognize what they are doing within the broader perspective outlined here; as well as take cognizance of the traditions and the reservoirs of potential common meaning that lie at the base of human experience that are available for renewal.

Pastoral counseling is in the process of rediscovering the soul. Through gaining a breadth of perspective as presented here, one can see that it is very difficult to separate the emotional and spiritual dimensions in counseling. To recognize that soul issues have a legitimate place in the counseling process is to help pastoral counseling achieve its unique identity.

CHAPTER 3

Holism in the Family: Implications for the Church from a Jungian Perspective

In our age of reasoning, it is much easier to think in terms of the rational analysis of minute details than to think in terms of the whole and its interdependent parts. In the specialization brought about by technological advances, our ability to think and experience reality holistically has been impaired. We do not often think in terms of open systems, because they are composed of complicated interchanges between interdependent structures that have complex processes. We would rather confine our thinking to small, manageable, closed systems that allow some degree of predictability.

The overemphasis upon parts as opposed to the whole can be seen in the dilemma of the American family today; a dilemma brought about by the increased emphasis on instant gratification and avoidance of pain by married couples and a decrease in emphasis on values that support satisfaction in pursuing unselfish goals for others.[1] Concern for the individual's own self-actualization, ambition, status, money, power, and achievement has become dominant at the expense of goals that focus on enabling others to become self-actualized.

Among the most tragic effects of this individualism and hedonism has been the submergence of the holistic function of the family, which is to fulfill each member's need for intimacy, fulfillment, commitment, growth, and development. To accomplish these goals in the family, people must seek not only their own fulfillment, but also the personal fulfillment of other family members; each must provide an atmosphere in which others can also grow.

Some attention will be given to the development of the overemphasis on individualism and its impact on the family. Increasingly the black family is becoming prey to what is taking place in all families. There will also be some attempt to suggest what can be done to influence this tendency to over-emphasize individualism, and how the ministry of the church can facilitate values that support holism in the family. Jungian psychology will be heavily relied upon for insights into ministry.

DEFINITIONS

No one who grew up in the American ethos can totally escape the individualistic influence; therefore, I possess many of the trappings of individualism that may emerge in this presentation from time to time. However, I would prefer to think that my orientation is focused more on the person than on the individual. The term *person* here refers to the understanding of the human being as a whole being whose growth and development take place in a social context. *Individual,* on the other hand, reflects more of the emphasis on self-sufficiency and personal achievement through an independent "boot-strap" philosophy.[2] Individualists see their own destiny as being in their own hands and are guided by self-interest, whereas personalists are concerned with reality as a society or collection of persons.[3]

When the focus is on the person rather than on the individual, it is possible to present a holistic view of people's needs. In the holistic view, the basic tendency, or inherent attribute and motivation, behind human growth and development, is the attempt of people to maximize both the expression of autonomy and the expression of harmony or communion. This emphasis on autonomy and communion can be found in the writings of Andras Angyal, David Bakan, and Otto Rank. It is also implied in the concept of the Afro-American unity of experience. Autonomy refers to one's ability to function apart from others. It implies being independent and having separate interests and goals. Communion, on the other hand, refers to a person's need to merge or join with others in interdependent relationships. In communion a person seeks a larger unit to be part of, and this need to merge is often satisfied by social structure, a cause, ideology, and religion.[4] Autonomy and communion are opposite forces, but they are simultaneously operative. The paradox is that both needs must find maximum expression to make life meaningful. Therefore, life must bring autonomy and communion into a harmonious tension so that a person can be whole.

Although modern marriage tends to be dominated by forces that emphasize autonomy at the expense of communion, today's marriage can provide an ideal atmosphere for autonomy and communion to find maximum expression. The development of the overemphasis upon autonomy will be explored in the next section.

CONTEMPORARY FAMILY

The overemphasis on autonomy in contemporary marriage is an expression of individualism, and the pursuit of instant gratification and the avoidance of pain. In an article entitled "Hedonism and the Family: Conflict in Values?" Lois and Paul Glasser point out that, in a world where consumerism is oriented toward gratification of immediate needs for pleasure, hedonism has combined with individualism to create a world where pleasure can only be achieved by seeking one's own ends. Such self-gratification is often accomplished at the expense of others. In this context, the goals of the family, unfortunately, have become those that maximize the individual's opportunities for pleasure and minimize the pain engendered by deprivation of immediate gratification. The results for the family of this overemphasis on autonomy have been an increasing failure in marriage, an alienation of individuals from the family, and a plethora of other related problems.[5]

Perhaps the most negative effect of individualism on the contemporary family is a rejection of the marriage norm by large numbers of people, even though statistics indicate that people are getting married at record rates. Nonetheless, there has been an assault on marriage. The rejection of the marriage norm has its origins in individualistic philosophy, according to Charles Frankel, professor of Philosophy and Public Affairs at Columbia University. He comments:

> The high value we have placed on individuality is one of the sources for the present tendency to put the family norm in question. As a norm, the family seems to require individuals to fit themselves to a mold, to do what John Stuart Mill thought they ought not to do—to accept as a rule of conduct the traditions and customs of other people. The family has, therefore, come to be seen as an instrument of institutional oppression. We can miss the point of much that goes by the name of "the new morality," . . . if we do not see that it is in its central tendencies simply an extension of well-established values, notably the value of individuality.[6]

The major conclusion of this article is that the present value placed on autonomy puts into question the family norm. In this context, values associated with communion are considered to be exploitive and oppressive. As a result, people's need for communion retreats to the unconscious and finds its expression through a search for absolutes and conformity among many people. Even many of the enthusiasts among those who pursue autonomy and individuality seek to meet their needs for communion through establishing organizations based on conformity to the norms of individualism. Many consciousness-raising groups whose slogans are fashioned from cloth of individualism are, in themselves, closed groups of people whose individuality has been subjugated to a conformity to group norms. The need for communion does not disappear, but it raises its head in the form of oppressive conformity. The real need is to bring autonomy and communion values into harmony within individuals.

THE FAMILY OF THE PAST

Individualism has a long history. The current wave goes back to the Industrial Revolution, and as a philosophy, must be regarded in the wider context of social, economic, and political happenings beginning at that time. Individualism is not the cause of many of the problems of contemporary family life, but it is one of many factors setting in motion the changes experienced by the family today. Among the other influential factors is the divorcing of the family from work and from the land.

Prior to the Industrial Revolution, work was associated with the home. Much of the work was centered in the home, and the father was closely involved in the life of the home and in the rearing of the children. However, the factory system changed all of this. One of the results has been that the authority of the male has been diminished. In the past, mothers held the family together with the authoritative male in the background.[7] His position of authority was unquestioned, but as a result of the Industrial Revolution, mothers were left on their own to hold the family together. There was no male authority to stand behind her authority. Thus, it was not the female or the feminist revolution that eroded the male domination in the home, but it was the Industrial Revolution. The family is crumbling at the foundation, not because of individual moral corruption, but because of the impact of industrialization and technology on family systems.

The disconnection between the family and work has also been accompanied by a schism between the family and the land. The Industrial Revolution pulled people off the farm in search of better jobs. Just as the cotton-picking machine made it unfeasible to maintain slave labor in the Confederate states, machines began to replace the small family farm with large farms operated by sophisticated machines. More and more small families and their farm help had to give up their land to find employment in the factories. Accompanying this slow process of disconnection has been a psychological feeling of uprootedness and insecurity. People, in actuality, have no real roots in the soil and are thrust into a world of strangers and urban impersonality.

The separating of the family from work and the land forms part of the economic and social background for the split between autonomy and communion. Philip Slater, in *Earthwalk,* maintained that people in simple communities or small villages, who are rarely exposed to people and relationships outside that village, feel themselves to be an organic and undetachable part of their immediate social and natural environment.[8]

In these communities autonomy and communion were not separated, but existed in juxtaposition with each other. When the Industrial Revolution occurred, with its emphasis upon mechanized values and goals, communion was relegated to a secondary position, and self-sufficient individualistic goals came into prominence. According to Philip Slater, what exists in our present-day culture is a schizoid phenomenon, in which the self is detached from its organic unity with the environment. In this context, autonomy and communion are diametrically opposed, and bringing them into harmony within individuals is very difficult to achieve.

Although autonomy and communion are split within persons, the woman in American society has been expected to sacrifice her autonomous striving for the sake of bringing a balance into the home. For many decades, society has placed all the demands for communion upon the female, while encouraging the male to pursue autonomous values in the world. Women now are reminding us that the family cannot be restored to primacy in our culture by their efforts alone. In order to regain its prominence in American culture today, the American family needs two adults of opposite sex who have achieved some degree of integration of autonomy and communion. The family cannot exist if either partner has to sacrifice autonomy or communion.

IMPLICATIONS FOR THE BLACK FAMILY

The black family from 1750 to 1925 was healthy in that it was an intact, well-defined structure with two parents as head, according to Herbert G. Gutman's *The Black Family in Slavery and Freedom 1750–1925.* However, significant changes in the black family took place after 1925. Gutman's thesis is that the significant changes in the black family took place between 1940 and 1970, when over four million blacks left the countryside for the cities. In 1940, over half the blacks lived in rural areas, and in 1965 four-fifths or them were in urban areas.[9] Thus, technology is having its impact on the black community and the family, because it was during this period that the black family began to decline. The black family is facing the same disabling technological pressures as all families, with less economic means to cope than other families.

The best example of how the technological pressures and individualistic values affect the black family is seen in the black extended family. Martin and Martin say:

> We are surprised, though, that so much talk of the adaptive capacities of the black family comes at a time when the black urban family is adapting less to the urban environment than ever before. The riots of the 1960's are evidence of that. Our study indicates that black kinship ties are threatened today more than ever before. Though extended family ties have been forged by economic necessity, paradoxically, it is the economic pressures (combined with the secular, materialistic, individualistic values) of urban life that today threaten to break up black kinship patterns.[10]

It is clear that the split between autonomy and communion cannot be avoided by the black family. The movement from the multi-generational extended family to the two-generational or one-generational nuclear family has been traced by Charles Stewart to the discontinuity of values from one generation to the next.[11] Communal values transmitted by family ties with the previous generation are largely eroding. Thus, the ability to sustain any values from one generation to the next in black families is being severely challenged by technology. The less we are rooted in the extended family the less we will feel the impact of tradition upon our lives. The more we are uprooted from past family traditions, the more individualism will be split from autonomy. Indeed, all families are undergoing the same dissolution due to the impact of technology.

A HOLISTIC MINISTRY OF FAMILIES

The task for ministry today is to help persons, the family, and the church to recover a meaningful value system that will help individuals, the family, and the church to bring balance to the opposites in their lives. Such a ministry must answer the following questions: (1) How can we regain a holistic value system in a culture that carries individualism to the extreme? (2) How do we bring the opposites of autonomy and communion into a helpful harmony in people's lives? (3) How do we recapture values that support people's growth as individuals while encouraging in them a commitment to the growth of others? (4) How can ministry facilitate self-actualization while enabling people to participate meaningfully in the lives of others?

In an attempt to answer these questions, I will draw from a model of ministry that reflects the significance of the unconscious as a reservoir of lost value that can be retrieved, given the right circumstances. Such an approach reflects the thinking of Carl Jung, who believed that enduring social values having the capacity to unite opposites do not themselves collapse when the cultural structures that carry these values falter as a result of technology. On the contrary, he thinks that lasting values supporting the union of opposites are found in the collective unconscious of humankind, which has become the storehouse for lost but enduring value. Summarizing Jung's position, Ira Progoff concludes:

> Fundamentally, then, the real continuity in history does not consist in the external forms of a civilization nor in the surface flow of events, but rather in the forces that are psychologically active in the depths of the people. While civilizations pass away, the propagation of people goes on; time accumulates within the human race even while the outward manifestations disappear.[12]

How can ministry tap this reservoir of meaning stored in the unconscious? Through the archetypal symbol, which is the form, or pattern, that transmits inherited ideas from the past through the unconscious.[13] The archetypes serve as the models for the formation of symbols of history. They are the stuff out of which images in dreams are constructed. Moreover, they are the vehicles through which values can be transmitted from generation to generation. Archetypes not only appear in dreams, but they are also evident in songs, poetry, dogma, ritual, and drama. The purpose of ministry is to release the power of the archetypal image in people's lives.

Archetypes have the power to unite opposites. From the Jungian point of view they are the most original, fundamental, and primordial expressions of life.[14] In fact, they represent the cosmos and the original condition out of which every person emerged. The archetypes also represent humanity's essential relation to structure of existence and the cosmos itself. As such, the archetypes help to put persons in touch with this reality or their original condition, and it is the regaining of this primary relationship that brings union of opposites. Restoration of one's essential relationship with the ground of being through the archetypes brings about the union of opposites *within* oneself. Archetypes, then, have the potential to unite people with the cosmos as well as uniting the opposites within the individuals themselves. Encountering the archetypes within one's life presents the potential for new being and the transformation of one's whole existence.

With the idea in mind that the archetype is an embodiment of the potential for a new existence, it is time to turn to the use of archetypes in ministry. In this light, the first task will be to examine the archetypes that appear in the life of the minister and to determine their significance for ministry.

Ministry begins with the person who is the actor in ministry. In the holistic model of ministry to families, the actor must be an integrated person in whom autonomy and communion co-exist. No matter what we preach or teach, people intuitively sense the nature of our internal maturity, and we need to spend some time developing our capacity to hold autonomy and communion in a harmonious tension.

This can be done in men by the recognition of the unconscious archetypal symbol of the *anima* that often appears in dreams. According to Jung, the anima is the inner "woman" in the man: the tender, emotional, feeling, erotic, and dependent side of his masculine personality. When a man is related to it, he is filled with loyalty, love, and relatedness to others, and it enables him to give emotional support to others.[15] Men often fear this influence because of the socialization into the masculine role, but such fear is unwarranted, and even dangerous. That is to say, the anima represents the possibility for communion within a man, and to ignore it cuts him off from an essential part of the self—a part of the self that helps him to be empathetic with women and to build significant relations to participate in the lives of others without fear of losing his self, and to construct an identity as an integrated person. In summary, the anima leads a man to communion with an important part of the self as well as with others.

While men have an inner woman, women have an inner "man," which Jung calls the *animus*. The animus is the force within the woman that propels her to be a separate, self-actualized, autonomous person, and enables her to develop a greater empathy with men. Through the growth of her own animus, she can experience a side of her personality that has been subjugated by culture and has been denied, and can realize potentials that have been reserved only for men for centuries.

To be integrated ministers, men must develop their anima, because it is in doing so that they discover their connectedness to the whole. Only when it is developed and brought into full relationship with other aspects of the conscious self, can a man become fully human. Women ministers must also develop the man within them in order to become integrated people possessing the capacity not only for communion, but also for agency and self-actualization. Experiencing of the anima and animus by men and women respectively brings wholeness and transformation to the personality.

The archetypes of the wise old man/wise old woman and the child are also significant to the wholeness of the pastor. The wise old sage is usually the guardian who appears in a dream, who gives protection from danger and guides the person to safety. This archetype often serves to bring wholeness by compensating for loss of contact with grandparents who have become dissociated from the nuclear family. The child-archetype is often a link with the past and is an attempt to bring one into contact with one's primordial or original state.[16] In addition, the appearance of the child-archetype in dreams signifies future change or the possibility of wholeness. Of course this potential for wholeness is linked with the past, and one's future personality becomes a synthesis of the present and past. Therefore, this archetype has the potential for uniting opposites and bringing healing or wholeness to the personality.[17]

Jungian archetypal theory has implications for ministry beyond that of developing integrated pastors. As indicated earlier, the power of the archetype to unite opposites is lodged within the collective unconscious. The process of dislodging the archetypes has been, according to Jung, the function of dogma, ritual, and creeds. These three forms are channels through which the community's original religious experiences were directed, and it was the archetype embodied in an image that helped to bring unity in people's lives.[18]

Because ritual and worship have embodied archetypal symbols in the past, corporate worship should not be ignored today for its potential for bringing integration and wholeness to people's lives. Encountering archetypes that have the potential for bringing unity could be one of the most important aspects of contemporary worship.

In addition to embodying values that unite opposites, traditional ritual also contained the wisdom of the ages as interpreted by the authorities of the church. When people participated in the traditional rituals, they were exposed to the values of the past that supported and contributed to value formation.

Participation in the rituals of the church is not enough to create integrated individuals today, however. Prior to the Reformation, ritual shielded many people from being overwhelmed by the tensions of opposites in their lives, but today's participation in the dogma, creeds, and rituals of the church will not have the same impact. Today people need to make conscious the archetypes operating in the life of the church. They need to work out ways that these symbols can nourish wholeness.

Participation in the ritualistic and worship life of the church may have lost its meaning for a good many people today, and the ministry of the church needs to be sensitive to the ingenious ways that the unconscious compensates for this loss. When creeds, rituals, and dogma lose their impact, a person does not lose the need to find symbols that unify life. In fact, the need for symbols is exacerbated. The unconscious takes over and seeks out symbols in the collective unconscious, which is the source of value that transcends cultural tradition.[19]

The dream is often the place where contemporary humanity finds the unifying symbol. For Jung, the images and symbols that appear in dreams are not mere words or concepts; they are often numinous. That is, encountering them and integrating them into consciousness can produce astonishing cures and religious conversions.[20] In this context, then, the image is not a concept, but "a piece of life" or "living matter" that has the power and energy to transform lives in much the same way that religious experience has. Thus the archetype performs a function akin to that of collective worship. The image is not private, emanating solely from within the person, but a vehicle for external truths originating from the cosmos, primordial experience, and human history. In this way, the image appearing in dreams is a resource for religious experience for contemporary humanity as well as a way of being united with the past.

The task of ministry is to enable people to encounter archetypes in their personal and corporate existence. The pastor must help persons to make these images appearing in dreams available to the conscious mind. A variety of methods exists for this, but the pastor's crucial task is to create an environment in which people feel at home exploring their inner life. For more specific methods for assisting the pastor in carrying out this form of ministry, consult the works of Morton Kelsey, particularly, *The Other Side of Silence: A Guide to Christian Meditation.*[21] Also consult the black conversion tradition found in *God Struck Me Dead.*[22]

To be consistent with the holistic approach, many of the methods for exploring the implications of archetypes encountered in worship and in dreams should be group methods. The methods in Kelsey's works can be adapted for groups without any difficulty. However, the pastor wishing to implement such a ministry might need to be thoroughly familiar with Jungian concepts, and to consult, on an ongoing basis, with someone who has a religious and therapeutic background.

Exploring archetypes encountered in the dreams of individuals and the rituals of the church has implications for family life. Group methods that help people in families and marriages identify archetypes that unify opposites need to be explored. Such images as anima and animus and their implications for producing improved marital relations need to be pursued. Moreover, the images of the wise old man/ wise old woman need to be examined in couple group settings for their potential in bringing enrichment to people's and families' lives.

In addition to the images already mentioned, there are other symbols that are appropriate for examination within the life of the small group, namely images of death and rebirth, regeneration, and nurturing. Representative symbols of such themes are the mandala (circle), the numbers three and four, nurturing mother, womb, cave, church, house, tree, water, and many others having to do with nature and animals. These images are often vehicles of numinous experiences; they reconcile opposites within the personality, and serve as spiritual guides for resolving theological issues (such as meaning in life).

In summary, archetypal theory in Jungian psychology has the potential of assisting a holistic ministry of the black church. It presents a novel way to counteract the pernicious influences of hedonism and individualism, as well as a path to unite autonomy and communion within persons. It points to a means of resurrecting values that have been lost due to the collapse of cultural systems, and it helps to provide a meaningful framework for people to be committed to the growth of others. This approach is new, but it must be seen as one of many; it may be helpful to some, but frightening to others. However, it is worth pursuing wherever there is openness to such an approach.

PART II

Pastoral Care and Counseling and the
Transmission of Values

CHAPTER 4

The Sociology of Pastoral Care and Counseling

One characteristic of modernity has been the fact that mediating structures are being pressured out of existence by technology. The family, the church, the voluntary association, the support system, and the subculture are mediating structures; while large political, economic, governmental, and educational structures are suprastructures. The importance of the mediating structures, according to Peter Berger, is that they contain the moral values that form a consensus for the behavior of individuals and society.[1] Because the supra-institutional structures are so far removed from concrete life, they are not suitable for maintaining general morality. Moreover, the individual has to depend on mediating structures to anchor identity and meaning. Thus, revitalizing mediating structures in the face of the pressures of technology is crucial for identity formation as well as for spiritual and moral growth.

The religious functionary has been the custodian of the religious and moral value structures throughout the history of society and the church. This is also true for the black pastor, who was custodian of the religious, moral, and spiritual world-view mediated to the community.[2] The pastor performed an important role in the mediating structure in nurturing and guiding persons in the religious world-view of

73

the church. This chapter is a sociological examination of the role of pastoral care and counseling in the church as a mediating structure throughout its history.

SOCIOLOGICAL THEORY

Sociology, in this chapter, will refer to discerning the social function of pastoral care and counseling within the church. According to Milton Yinger, religion can serve a variety of functions. *Function* here means the organic processes that contribute to the maintenance of an organism.[3] In this context, religion can function as an integrator of all dimensions of society on the social level, and provide meaning that integrates lives on the personal level. Thus religion can serve to promote social and personal integrity.

Pastoral care and counseling are agents of the social and personal functions of religion from a sociological perspective. Theologically, pastoral care and counseling are response patterns to the love shown by Jesus in caring service to others. Sociologically, this caring response is done in a moral and spiritual context that informs the scope and process of the caring. The function of pastoral care and counseling is to bring the "sacred cosmos" to bear upon the person or family for the purpose of maintaining physical and emotional integrity.

What is the *sacred cosmos*? It is a sociological construct that refers to an objective social reality that transcends the person, but is essential to the person's growth as a social, moral, and religious being. It is part of a social world-view or an objective system of meaning, in which an individual is integrated into a coherent social system, and it enables the person to find his or her place in relationship to others, find order and meaning for personal existence, and avenues to the truly transcendent.

Thus, the sacred cosmos is very much a part of the mediating structure, especially of the church. The sacred cosmos is the highest symbolic order within the world-view.[4] It provides a framework for interpreting significant events

PASTORAL COUNSELING AND SPIRITUAL VALUES

and values for informing conduct. It also has, as a part of its tradition, doctrines and codified sacred texts and commentaries. It also is fixed in liturgy and the specialists appointed to reenact the liturgy. "The doctrine is transmitted and interpreted by an official body of experts in a manner that is binding for the layman."[5] The pastoral counselor is such an expert.

It must be added that the sacred cosmos is related significantly to the concepts of the collective unconscious and symbols emerging from the psyche. The sacred cosmos is the codification and systemization of people's original religious and social experiences. Symbols emerging from the collective unconscious were the original subjective experiences that gave rise to the sacred social cosmos. The sacred cosmos arose as a result of the objectification of individuals' original encounter with the transcendent on a subjective level. Thus, the sacred cosmos is very much related to the soul experiences of individuals and of small communities, which have been codified and have social continuity through shared community symbols.

In summary, the pastoral counselor's sociological function is to bring the sacred cosmos to bear upon the lives of people and families. To do this would greatly contribute to the welfare and integrity of the individual and the family.

THE SACRED COSMOS AND MODERNITY

Since the sacred cosmos is part of a mediating structure, it, too, has been influenced by technology. The major thesis of this chapter is that modern-day pastoral counseling is a child of secularity and reflects the breakup of the sacred cosmos. This section will explore this thesis through the use of the sociological terms *secularity* and *modernization*.

Secularity refers to the weakening of the plausibility of the religious perceptions of reality. God and the religious explanations of reality are removed from the center of the community's life and replaced by a scientific image of reality.

Secularity refers to the removal of the transcendent from the center of life.[6]

Modernization is the force behind the secularization process. It is "the transformation of the world brought about by technological innovations."[7] It is characterized by the following: the removal of the person from society, the removal of institutions from concrete reality, the disintegrating of love from its social context, and the distancing of language from the behavior it describes. The result of this pervasive abstraction is a demarcation of reality into meaningless separate entities. The spiritual is separated from the nonspiritual, the rational from the irrational, the sacred from the secular, and the person from community. As the abstraction increases, the person becomes more isolated from those around him or her, and narcissism and extremes of individualism divorced from community take place.

Pastoral care and counseling have been influenced by this pervasive abstractionism and have, therefore, given up the sacred cosmos for a secular one. The result has been an identity crisis in which pastoral care and counseling have over-identified with secular forms of counseling at the expense of their task relative to the sacred cosmos. Up until the last ten years, they have generally lost touch with their sacred trust. The next section will examine the historical context of this sacred trust.

PASTORAL CARE AND COUNSELING IN HISTORICAL PERSPECTIVE

The Premodern Period

The premodern period is the period that preceded the technological and industrial revolution. The end of the premodern period is usually associated with the scientific revolution beginning in the fifteenth and sixteenth centuries, with such notable names as Copernicus, Galileo, and Newton. In religion, the Protestant Reformation marked the end of the premodern period and the beginning of the

Enlightenment and the Age of Reason, which marks the shift to the modern period.

The task of this section is to examine the role of pastoral care in the premodern period. In order to approach this task, I will draw upon the work of William A. Clebsch and Charles P. Jaekle, *Pastoral Care in Historical Perspective.*

Pastoral care in the premodern period performed the sociological function of socialization. Socialization is the consistent induction of an individual into an objective and real world of values of a society or a particular sector of it.[8] In its use here, socialization refers to inducting persons into the sacred cosmos that existed in the earlier church and in the Roman Catholic Church in the premodern period. Thus, when the carer during this period performed the roles of healing, sustaining, guiding, or reconciling, he did it within a specific social and psychological context of a sacred cosmos that helped the person understand the nature of reality, his or her place in it, and how to govern himself or herself accordingly. The sacred world-view also helped people in need to understand peculiar as well as non-peculiar internal and external events taking place in their lives. The sacred cosmos was an objective structure that could be made concrete and relevant to the lives of individuals. When it was made relevant, it successfully helped induct and *integrate* people into the sacred social order.

The socialization function of pastoral care can be seen clearly when one looks at the periods of history when socialization through guidance was the dominant form of pastoral care. These periods include the fourth century, fifth century, and the eleventh and twelfth centuries. Guiding can be seen clearly in other periods of premodern pastoral care, but the socialization during the fourth, fifth, eleventh, and twelfth centuries is unmistakable.

During the fourth century, the persecution that had characterized much of the early church's experience had ended. Constantine came to the throne, and one of his first decrees was to make Christianity the official religion of the Roman Empire. The church performed the sociological function of unifying and integrating all life, and a practical theology was developed that informed the major areas of communal living.

According to Clebsch and Jaekle, the dominant form of pastoral care during this period was guiding.[9] That is, clergy sought to help people make confident decisions based on a prior or pre-existing understanding of reality, independent of the person and the religious functionary. This is called inductive guiding, or the induction of a person into a pre-existing world-view with the expectation that meaning will be brought to the life of the person. Thus, the occasion for pastoral guidance was also an opportunity for socialization.

The socialization function through pastoral guidance was also a part of the fifth-century Christian Church. This was a period of time characterized by the spread of the faith to Northern Europe, known as the Dark Ages; and pastoral guidance was purely for the purpose of socialization. That is, pastoral guidance became the vehicle through which the sacred cosmos, now infused intricately with the Roman civilization, was brought to bear upon those persons in northern Europe who, at that time, were considered heathens and barbarians.

In the eleventh and twelfth centuries, the cohesion of the church and society was firmly established. Therefore, the guiding ministry, which was basically the transmission of the sacred cosmos, was carried on without much difficulty. Pastoral guiding performed a maintenance role and helped keep the sacred cosmos firmly intact.

THE MODERN PERIOD OF PASTORAL CARE

The Protestant Reformation was an expression of many social and religious forces in society during the sixteenth century. Although one cannot directly trace the beginning of the modern period to Martin Luther, his efforts are a good paradigm for understanding the forces leading to the modern period. For example, Luther's challenge of the sacred cosmos was a manifestation of forces in a variety of arenas that were challenging the exclusive custodial rights of the church over the sacred cosmos. What Luther did was to bring trends to full expression that were developing in many sectors of society.

The foundation of the modern period resulted from attacks on the rights of exclusive custody of the sacred cosmos. The exclusive right of the clergy to mediate this cosmos was questioned. Luther's successful doctrine of the priesthood of all believers opened the door wide so that all persons became custodians of the sacred world-view. Thus the foundation was laid for the individual to have direct access to God without the custodian's hindering. The Protestant Reformation, the scientific revolution, and the emergence of the dominance of reason disrupted the church's dominance in interpreting the nature of reality. The door was opened to nonreligious or secular interpretations of reality as well as to pluralism or competing sacred and nonsacred world-views.

The response of pastoral care to the disruption of the sacred cosmos during the Reformation was the same as in earlier periods of the seventeenth and eighteenth centuries, but it was much different in the nineteenth and twentieth centuries. In the seventeenth and eighteenth centuries, pastoral care was still focused on socialization of persons into the sacred cosmos; however, the socialization occurred in diverse religious movements that had strong personalities as leaders, rather than the socialization of all persons into a church/state religion. The Puritan experiment, for example, was focused on inducting persons into a religious world-view while avoiding the entrapments of the secular world.

In the nineteenth and twentieth centuries, pluralism and secularization had their triumphant impact upon the sacred cosmos. The mediating structures that were the real custodians of the sacred cosmos began to give way to the technological revolution, and there resulted a growing gap between suprastructures and the individual. The soil for privatism had been cultivated and the seeds were germinating. *Privatism* here means the selection of one's own private religion or sacred cosmos from a number of competing values systems without institutional support.[10] The stage was set for narcissistic self-indulgence and individual hedonism.

It was in this social context that pastoral counseling, as a specific dimension of pastoral care, emerged. The socialization function continued in pastoral counseling, but it was no longer inducting persons into a sacred cosmos. Rather, pastoral counseling became a means of socializing persons into a secularized psychological world-view.[11]

In the modern context, those who would perform pastoral counseling have three models to follow. There is the traditional application of the sacred cosmos to the person's problems, based upon denominational and local church tradition. There is the other extreme of borrowing one's assumptions, concepts, and methods from other professions, such as medical psychiatry and social work. The third alternative is to borrow from the behavioral sciences and correlate them with the sacred cosmos, keeping the best of both worlds. One can find all three responses characterizing pastoral counselors during the twentieth century. Yet the adoption of behavioral science approaches without applying theological norms has been a real danger in pastoral counseling. It has led to an identity crisis which has contributed to the secularization of the profession of pastoral counseling. The secularization can be seen in the following trends: (1) the adoption of educative guidance and rejecting of inductive guidance, (2) the split of pastoral counseling from the parish, (3) the development of specialized skills and theory derived from secular disciplines, (4) the abandonment of theological sources, and (5) the dominance of the one-to-one models of counseling.

In these five trends, the abstract and privatistic forces of modernity are at work. For example, educative guiding seeks to draw upon the individual for guidance rather than upon some pre-existing world-view. Thus, some aspects of pastoral counseling support privatization. Second, the dominance of the one-to-one model during this period reflects the abstraction of the individual from the social context of family and support systems. This abstraction tendency can also be seen in the divorcing of pastoral counseling from the parish and from its theological sources.

Not all pastoral counseling models are victims of modernity, yet the influence of modernization on many models of pastoral counseling cannot be ignored. In fact, there has been an almost total abandonment of inductive guidance in pastoral care. Some models neglect theology, while others do not. Some counselors adopt the professional models of psychiatry and clinical psychology, while others attempt to keep close contact with denominational and church contexts of pastoral counseling. The agenda of pastoral counseling has been greatly influenced by the forces of technology.

THE POST-MODERN PERIOD

The onset of the 1970s marked the end of the modern period and the commencement of the post-modern period. This period is characterized by three trends. The first is a disenchantment with scientific, utopian solutions to ultimate concerns. The second is a resurgence of interest in the transcendent and the sacred, and the third is a concern for the whole person and his or her context.

The disenchantment with scientific solutions to human problems is a result of misplaced loyalty to science. There were unrealistic expectations of the power of science to perform miracles that might make suffering, pain, and oppression disappear. Although people can live longer as a result of scientific discoveries, misery and pain are still at hand. The deeper questions of life relative to ultimate meaning persist even in the face of scientific discovery. The scientific world, so far at least, has not been able to replace theology. Peter Berger says, "I am impressed by the intrinsic inability of secularized world views to answer the deeper questions of whence, whither, and why."[12]

There is also a renewed interest in the transcendent. Berger points out that when tradition has been challenged to the point that there are no norms, convictions are shattered, institutions are tottering, and rootlessness and disorientation are rampant, history shows that there is a resurgence of interest in religion.[13] Thus, we are entering an age wherein the reversal of the secularization process is beginning. Berger further states that there is an instinct for the transcendent in human nature closely akin to the Freudian concept of drives, and like Freud's conceptualization of repression, the repressed spiritual dimension cannot be turned away and ignored forever.[14]

Another countermodernizing trend is the movement away from isolating people from their context. This movement can be seen in the use of systems theory in almost all areas of life, from psychotherapy to public policy-making. Systems theory is an attempt to understand human behavior in a contextual, holistic, and corporate way. The roots of this theory extend back to Hegel in the nineteenth century, but did not gain prominence in America until after World War II, through the work of an Austrian biologist at State University of New York, Ludwig Von Bertalanffy. His views challenged the mechanistic and cause-and-effect models of behavior, and instituted in their place teleological-circular-causal, contextual, and vitalistic models.[15] This theory supports one of the trends against modern abstraction.

The three countermodernizing trends noted above can be seen in the present literature on pastoral counseling. There are five emerging trends that need to be noted in pastoral counseling: (1) the renewed interest in the historical roots of pastoral care and counseling; (2) the resurgence of interest in mystery and transcendence; (3) the emergence of a holistic understanding of persons; (4) the coming of age of the identity of the pastoral counselor; and (5) the rediscovery of pastoral guidance. No attempt will be made here to develop these five trends, only a brief paragraph given citing recently published material.[16]

The historical interest in pastoral care can be seen in Don S. Browning's *The Moral Context of Pastoral Care* and in Clebsch and Jaekle's *Pastoral Care in Historical Perspective*.

With regard to the importance of the transcendent and mysterious, the works of Morton Kelsey have been of interest to pastoral counselors. The systems approach to pastoral counseling can be seen in the works of Mansell Pattison, Charles Gerkin, and Charles Stewart. The theological concern is evidenced in the works of William Hulme, William Willimon, John Cobb, and Charles Gerkin. The prominence of pastoral guidance is evidenced in the work of Don S. Browning.

It is the work by Browning that highlights the importance of the church as mediating structure. Even though there is no consistent sacred cosmos, every church has an obligation to help people develop a personal philosophy and theology of life that informs their behavior. How this is done will be the subject of the next several chapters, with special reference to pastoral care and counseling.

CONCLUSION

Pastoral counseling is in a better position today to make a contribution to the black church because of the counter-modernization trends. It holds out means of developing the mediating structures by drawing upon systems theories, as well as helping pastoral counselors deal with the context in which black Christians live. Pastoral counseling will become more attractive to many black Christians when it has its theological identity together as well as its moral guidance approach. Thus the trends in pastoral counseling are making it more relevant to the black Christian experience.

CHAPTER 5

Pastoral Care and Support Systems

There is an increased interest within the local church in models of caring that complement and facilitate the use of the church's traditional resources. There is also a growing dissatisfaction among the clergy with psychoanalytic models of pastoral counseling that ignore the strengths of tradition, and there is a corresponding effort to find other, more appropriate, models. An alternative model of caring for local churches is needed that can help the church utilize its reservoir of values and resources. In this way the local church can become a better mediating structure between the individual and wider society and assist people in nomos building.

Historically, pastoral counseling has functioned in a manner that has alienated it from the local church. For example, very few members, about 15 percent in fact, of the American Association of Pastoral Counselors are local-church pastors. Most of the members in this organization work in pastoral counseling centers or as special chaplains in hospitals and the military. One of the limitations of the pastoral counseling movement is that it has not spoken to the needs of local churches, and this is reflected in the make-up of the American Association of Pastoral Counselors. Morris Taggart, in an article entitled, "The Professionalization of the Parish Pastoral Counselor," comments on the irrelevance of pastoral counseling to the local parish. He says:

A very serious effect of the situation we are all in is the growing sense of there being a gap between the counseling concerns of parish ministers and the overall development of the field. Parish ministers attending summer workshops in pastoral counseling frequently complain that the material offered at such workshops, as well as much of what appears in the books and journals, appears to be aimed more at the specialist pastoral counselor rather than the parish clergy. These clergy from the parish insist that the special issues associated with doing counseling in a parish setting are either not dealt with in much of the writings or are shrugged off. . . . In a word, professional pastoral counselors are being experienced as irrelevant to the special needs of the parish clergy as are psychiatrists and psychologists.[1]

Indeed, there are problems in the relationship between pastoral counseling and the kinds of problems in local churches. There are many reasons for this apparent difficulty. Among the reasons are an identity problem among pastoral counselors that has manifested itself in the pastoral counselor's identification with psychiatrists and psychologists, the inadequacy of the one-to-one medical model of psychoanalysis for understanding multiple problems in parish settings, and the failure of the pastoral counselor to use the unique resources that the local church has to offer in the field of mental health.[2] All three of the reasons are related to each other; they are aspects of the same problem. These reasons reflect the fact that pastoral counseling has relied more upon secular disciplines for its norms and procedures than upon the church's rich tradition. Because of this, pastoral counseling has overlooked many historical therapeutic resources within the Christian faith; namely, the caring community, the worship tradition, the prayer tradition, and the ethical value tradition of the church. All of these traditions are resources the pastoral counselor can use to aid the growth of a person.

I am not suggesting that pastoral counseling ignore the

secular disciplines. On the contrary, I am suggesting that pastoral counseling, and especially pastoral care, select only those models and methods from the behavioral sciences that serve the ends of the mission of the church as it has been historically conceived. The behavioral science models, when used, must enable pastoral care and counseling to utilize the traditional resources of the Christian church for ministry. This counseling must serve the communal needs as well as the individual needs; it must serve spiritual needs as well as psychological needs; it must help one to unite with one's Creator, as well as help one regain mental health.

Because the one-to-one medical model of psychiatry has been inadequate by itself for local parishes, I would like to suggest an alternative; namely, the community mental health model. The community mental health model attempts to prevent mental illness in the community through addressing the multifaceted forces that provoke or ameliorate a mental disorder.[3] This model is valuable to the pastor because it deals with the many factors in the environment that may aid or hinder people's growth,[4] whereas the psychoanalytic model deals primarily with the internal life of the counselee and the interpersonal relationship between the counselee and the counselor. The community mental health model is also a way to penetrate the lives of people living in the community in order to build up and influence the environmental factors that might contribute positively to people's mental health. It is concerned with the total community rather than the individual.

My own experience as a pastoral consultant and my work as a pastor and seminary professor have taught me the value of the community mental health approach. I think this approach has direct relevance to the local church because it deals with (1) normal rather than pathological needs of people, (2) prevention, (3) whole populations, not just the individual, (4) the kinds of environmental factors that influence the mental health of people, and (5) facilitates the use of the traditional caring-resources in the church. Among the factors that influence mental health are support systems.

Because the local church is a caring community, support systems theory in community mental health is a natural model to help move pastoral counseling and care away from the medical model and toward the utilization of the church's natural and traditional resources. We will now explore the relevance of support systems to pastoral care.

WHAT ARE SUPPORT SYSTEMS?

Before we define support systems, it would be helpful to define pastoral care. Pastoral care is the ministry of the church; it brings to bear on the person and family in crises the total resources of the church. Pastoral counseling, on the other hand, is a specialized form of pastoral care that usually confines the therapeutic role of the minister to persons, families, and small groups. In pastoral counseling, the major resource for caring is the minister; whereas pastoral care not only utilizes the minister but also utilizes many of the church's traditional and natural resources.

When pastoral care is defined as "the bringing to bear of the total resources of the church upon people and families in crises," the role of support systems in pastoral care must be considered. Support systems theory assumes that the arena of healing in people's lives is the supportive community,[5] and not just a therapeutic relationship between doctor and patient. In this model, the agent of the healing is the supportive community; in pastoral care, the healing agent in the church is the caring community. The healing forces in the local church (from the perspective of support systems theory) are the caring relationships that exist in families, extended families, peer groups, friendship and fellowship circles, prayer and Bible study groups, and informal, face-to-face encounters. Beyond their interpersonal aspects, support systems are also vehicles through which God's redemptive love moves to unite God and his people. Support systems are channels for healing in crisis situations as well as for God's redemptive love. Thus they are mediating and nomos-building structures.

A support system is defined as a pattern of continuous ties with significant others that help the person maintain emotional and physical integrity during crisis periods. These systems help people in a crisis to maintain their health and comfort, reinforce their own capacity to cope with crisis situations, provide them with community validation for their identity and self-worth, satisfy a person's need for caring relationships, and help them express their emotions and control their impulses.[6]

There are religious support systems that not only help maintain a person's emotional and physical integrity, but also help to bring religious resources to the person in crisis. Religious support systems give people in crisis an opportunity to identify with friends, provide opportunities for joint allegiance to shared views and values about God, provide a tradition of ritual practices to help deal with crises such as birth and death, provide a cohesive reference group for controlling and directing impulses, provide religious literature that works to strengthen their understanding about what is happening to them and how God is working to be present with them in their predicament, and provide an enabling faith in God that gives meaning to life and hope for a better future.[7]

The question may arise: Does a person really need the help of support systems? Psychological studies have shown that people are open to the influence of others during crisis periods more than at any other period in their lives.[8] In crisis periods, people face problems in their lives they cannot solve by the usual problem-solving mechanisms. During these periods, they turn to others for help in the resolution of their crises, and it is at this point of crisis that the church has opportunities to intervene in people's lives to help them solve their problems. The proper employment of support systems in the local church during crisis periods can be very therapeutic.

Support systems satisfy many personal needs in a crisis situation. People in crisis need a buttress against social disorganization. They need help in mastering threatening situations in life; they need consistent feedback from others about what is expected of them in a crisis; they need assistance with crisis coping tasks and an evaluation of how well they are doing in their performance of these tasks; and they need a socially accepted outlet for emotions and feelings. Proper employment and use of the support system resources in a local church helps meet the needs of people in crisis situations.

A CASE STUDY

At this point it will be helpful to study a case that demonstrates the use of support systems during the bereavement of a loved one. The case is that of an African pastor of a black Congregational Church in Boston, Massachusetts. Because of his African heritage, he was very sensitive to the kinship and community ties of the people in his congregation, and he was always looking for opportunities to use the natural relationship between people of his church in pastoral care. The case study is an excellent demonstration of how a pastor can help the person in crisis by using caring support systems in pastoral care.

The pastor was concerned about a black male who was in his late fifties. He was dying of cancer. Prior to the discovery of the cancer, the parishioner had sustained injuries in a serious car accident. Initially, the parishioner's illness was linked to complications associated with the car accident. During the man's convalescence, however, it was discovered that he was terminally afflicted with cancer of the liver. When the parishioner was told of his disease and the negative prognosis, he responded with disbelief. He would not accept the doctor's findings; rather, he insisted that his illness was only the result of the car accident and that he would return home and to work in a short time.

The dying man was not alone during this difficulty. His immediate family consisted of two younger sisters who lived in the Boston area. These sisters had good relationships with their brother and felt they had obligations toward him, especially during his illness. They were very upset about his illness and were equally concerned about his inability to accept the fact that he was dying.

The dying parishioner also had an older sister in the deep South with whom he had a very close relationship. This closeness was far greater than that with his other two sisters and was directly related to the fact that the older sister baby-sat for him during his childhood.

The dying man's relationship with the pastor was a comfortable one. The pastor had visited him periodically in the hospital from the onset of the hospitalization. The pastor was concerned about the dying man's inability to accept the fact of his impending death and expressed this concern to the sisters. They failed to help their brother accept his death, just as the pastor had failed. The pastor and sisters began to talk, and they then discovered that the dying man would probably be more open to his older sister than he was to them. Therefore, the pastor sent for this older sister. They found that the dying man talked very freely with the older sister, and as a result, was able to accept the fact that he was dying.

The pastor also contacted the man's adult son. The father and son were estranged, but they were reconciled by the pastor's efforts.

The dying man was in his second marriage, but he was estranged from his second wife. However, when she learned of her husband's illness from the pastor, she was a great deal of help to her husband during his final days. She visited him quite often and tried to make things very comfortable for him.

Finally the man died. The minister continued his role by preparing the family for the funeral. The pastor found that the family's participation in preparing the funeral service stimulated them to express their feelings about their beloved brother, husband, and father. The pastor found that this process enabled them to review their lives with the dying man, and this helped them grieve for their loved one.

The pastor also had laypersons in the congregation, trained to be a help to people in crises. Many of his parishioners were from the South and West Indies, and many of them knew, because of cultural tradition, what to do when people were in crises, especially the grief crisis. The pastor built upon this cultural tradition in his training of the congregation.

ANALYSIS OF CASE

Before examining the way the pastor used the support systems to facilitate the ministry of the church to the man and his family in a crisis, it is important to examine the psychological dimensions of dying and bereavement as presented in the case.

Elisabeth Kübler-Ross has pointed out that during the dying process it is very important that the dying person accept the fact that he or she is dying.[9] In facing the fact that he or she is dying, she or he can talk about it with others, and in the process, discover new dimensions of life in spite of death.

Notice how the dying parishioner denied the fact that he was dying. He protested that he was not dying. The fact that the man was denying his approaching death should not be a cause of great concern. Elisabeth Kübler-Ross has stated that the first stage of accepting death is denial.[10] In this case the man really denied he was dying; thus, he could not accept it. He protested that he would return to work. Fortunately, the pastor realized that denial is the first stage of acceptance of one's death, and the pastor respected the man's protest.

Acceptance of one's death in the dying process is very important, because it is so necessary for the person to find meaning in life in spite of death. Death is scary, indeed, but it becomes less so if we are able to talk about it with others. More than this, we begin to realize that meaning in life—the ability to discover new dimensions in human encounters—is possible up until the very time of death. This reminds me of the words of Jesus, "I came that they might have life and have it more abundantly" (John 10:10 RSV). Even when we accept the fact that we are dying, God has created the world in such a fashion that new meaning and purpose in life are possible, even when death is going to lay its icy hands upon us.

In addition to the dynamics of dying, there are personal dynamics of bereavement. There are certain psychological tasks that must be accomplished during bereavement. *Bereavement* is the sudden cessation of social interraction.[11] It elicits negative emotions and the mourner exhibits a characteristic syndrome following the loss of a loved one. During the process of grief, the grief-sufferer must give up the lost object. This means the person must accept the fact that his or her loved one is dead, in order to then be able to turn to life again. The process of bereavement involves reviewing the relationship with the deceased, expressing feelings of loss and abandonment, arranging one's life in order to live without the loved one, and working on the tasks of burial. In normal circumstances, the whole grief process takes about six weeks.

The grief process in the family of the dying man was interesting, because it was a classic example of anticipatory grief—the family of the dying man had an opportunity to work on the tasks of grieving prior to the death of their loved one. The family had accepted the fact that their beloved would die. Because they had accepted this fact early, they experienced many of the feelings of loss and abandonment before he died. More important, they were able to share these feelings with each other and with their beloved. When the actual death came, much of their feelings had been worked through, and the actual grieving period was not as long as it would have been otherwise.

In the grief work I have done in my ministry, many of the people express regret about the untimely death of their beloved. They say they had so much to tell the person, but now it is no longer possible. However, in anticipatory grief, people have an opportunity to say whatever they wish to their loved one. Fortunately, this was possible in the case study I have presented.

Now that we have sketched briefly the dynamics of dying and grief, let us look at the role the pastor performed in utilizing the support systems during this period.

The support-systems task of the pastor during the crises of dying and bereavement is to enable the support systems to provide healing resources. In the case of the dying parishioner, this meant enabling the support systems to meet his needs for loving companions to the end, as well as to help him accept the fact that he was dying. In terms of the bereaved family, the role of the pastor was to stimulate the resources in the family itself and to use the resources of the church to help the family.

The pastor first brought the healing resources in the dying man's family to his aid. The dying parishioner was largely uncommunicative about his condition with the pastor. The pastor tried to help the man open up by bringing his two sisters in to talk with him. He was not able to respond to them, however, so the pastor sent for the man's older sister. In this context, the pastor was a support systems enabler. As such, he attempted to use the family to help the dying man receive the kind of companionship he needed and to help him accept his impending death. This use of the family support system by the pastor enabled the dying man to discuss his fears about dying with someone he loved, to renew old relationships, and to create new ones. Creating new relationships was made possible when the pastor made the effort by bringing the man's son to visit with him in the hospital. The man and his son had not talked for several years. The pastor, as a support systems enabler, facilitated their reunion. Not only did they get together, but they were also able to share their real concerns, and forgive mistakes made in the past. Of course, it is always helpful to the dying person to have attempted to correct difficulties and misunderstandings with loved ones before death. This enables the dying person to accept death more easily. It also helps the mourner to grieve. In the case study, all of this happened because the pastor was sensitive to support systems surrounding the dying man.

After the parishioner died, the pastor used the support systems resources to assist the family through the bereavement process. Although the family had grieved prior to the parishioner's death, the death brought with it additional feelings of loss in the family. In this context the pastor used the funeral service preparation as a support system resource. The pastor felt that having the family participate in the actual building of the funeral service would enable them to review their life and relationships with the deceased. He thus used the funeral service preparation to continue the process of bereavement.

The pastor also used the wake to facilitate the grief process. He structured the wake in such a way that those who were not able to attend the family planning session had an opportunity to share their feelings at the wake. The pastor also used appropriate scripture and music at the wake, which further facilitated the grief process.

The pastor also used the caring community within the church to aid in the grief process. In this church, custom dictated the way mourners should act. This was particularly true of the parishioners from the South and from the West Indies. The pastor used these customs as opportunities to help the grief-stricken family. He helped the parishioners to be in the right places for the bereaved family. If there was need of assistance in cooking or dispersion of personal effects of the deceased, people were made available for this from the church. Moreover, deacons were trained and supervised by the pastor for helping families in bereavement, as well as with other needs.

The African pastor was acutely sensitive to families and people in crisis. He was able to take many opportunities presented to him to use support systems resources in his pastoral care. His rich cultural background from Africa assisted him in the mobilization of support systems resources. Thus, when crises arose, he was able to involve his whole church in the ministry to the families in crisis.

CONCLUSION

Through the use of support systems in the local church, it is possible to add new dimensions of meaning to the lives of people in crises. During crises, people naturally look for assistance from others. They are open to the influence of others. Proper use of support systems within families and within the church can introduce the suffering person to new levels of relationships. In the case study presented earlier, the dying man discovered that it was possible to experience meaningful relationships in spite of impending death.

The possibility for creating new meaning through the use of support systems became a reality both for the dying man and for the members of the support system. Those who participate in support systems, especially during bereavement, come to the realization that bereavement and grief are temporary, although death is permanent. The grief-stricken feel as though part of them has died, but soon learn that a recommitment to life is possible. Those who are in the support system descend into hell, literally, with the person and family in crisis. But they arise victoriously when the grief process is over. They arise with new meaning in their lives. In spite of the tragedies that exist in life, there is the possibility to affirm the value of life. "O death where is thy victory? O death where is thy sting?" (I Cor. 15:55 RSV).

Another implication of the case study for the local church has to do with educating the laity for its caring ministry. The pastor trained his deacons for what they needed to do during crisis periods in the congregation. We pastors cannot expect people to know automatically what they should do when they are called upon in crisis situations. People must be trained about the various needs people have in crises and how they can help meet these needs.

An important implication of the case study has to do with the role of the minister. The pastor in the case study has always looked for ways to help the caring community accomplish the healing. The more I engage in group counseling the more I realize that groups can do so much more than I can alone. Yes, ministers do have a role in crisis intervention and counseling, but I feel support systems should also be used in crisis intervention.

The final implication of the case study has to do with the value of support systems theory for the local church. Unlike traditional psychoanalytic theory, support systems theory fits in naturally with the structure of the local church. It helps the pastor more effectively use the healing resources of the church in the funeral service, the caring community, and theology. Thus, the support systems theory approach to community mental health is a better option for the local church than the traditional one-to-one approach. It helps to build the value of the local church as a mediating structure linking meaning of the past with present crises.

CHAPTER 6

Family Dynamics and Value Stabilization

INTRODUCTION

Improving family dynamics has an effect on the transmission of values. The family, as a mediating structure of
values from generation to generation, must function well
internally to assist in the stabilization of values. The
correlation between the transmission of value and family
dynamics will be examined in this chapter. First, the
theoretical and theological foundations for understanding
the value transmission function of the family will be
explored; and second, the family dynamics that facilitate
nurturing family relationships will be examined.

ASSUMPTIONS

Five assumptions are fundamental to this chapter. The
first assumption is that families as units can cope with a
variety of social and external pressures when the internal
family coping mechanisms are adequate. The second is that
families are mediating structures for God's love and grace.
The third assumption is that caring relationships within the
family set the foundation for the child's ability to establish an
identity and to find meaning. The fourth assumption is that

the quality of family relationships can lessen the impact of technology upon the family. The fifth assumption is that establishing caring relationships across generational lines is crucial in the transmission of important values from one generation to the next.

In Part I, the impact of the technological revolution on the family was examined in some detail. The analysis primarily dealt with families in general, but the black family did not escape the pervasive influence of technology. From 1940 to the present time, the disruptive influences of modernization have had their impact on the black family. This has been demonstrated by the detailed work of Gutman.[1] Therefore, modern black family patterns are less influenced by the historical forces of slavery than they are affected by contemporary issues such as lack of job skills, unemployment, inflation, and other issues that are related to modernization.

While some of the major influences affecting the family are social and external to the family, pastoral counseling with families and married couples assumes that the family and marriage systems are not totally determined by social and external forces. In fact, the family and marriage institutions have within them a tremendous potential for a range of choices to be actualized. The family system and marital resources, if tapped, could assist families and married couples in choosing appropriate problem-solving patterns in the face of tremendous social pressures. The assumption is not that families are incapable of responding in the face of large social problems, but that the family and marriage resources can be brought to bear on crucial problems if stimulated by other caring people.

The family and the marriage are important reservoirs of strength and healing in the midst of urban and technological society. The resources of the family, however, are often hidden and dormant, waiting to be awakened. This resource can be awakened in a variety of ways, including economic, educational, and political approaches. There are also educational and religious approaches that can tap and strengthen family resources. Rather than exploring these varied approaches, the purpose here is to develop a pastoral counseling approach to families, recognizing that it is only one of many ways to stimulate the resources inherent in black families. In short, the emphasis is on using pastoral counseling to strengthen the family as a mediating structure capable of transmitting meaning to its members.

Stimulating the resources within families through pastoral counseling must be seen, for our purposes, from a Christian perspective. The family and marriage are viewed as systems of relationships between a husband and wife and their offspring, which form a caring matrix through which God's love can be mediated to the family members. In this view, the foundation of all the resources for dealing with contemporary problems in modern life is God, and caring relationships within the family serve as vehicles through which divine resources are made available to family members.

Also important in the Christian understanding of marriage is the recognition that families serve as the primary shapers of reality and meaning for newborn children. The quality of care within the home influences the way the child will become oriented to reality, develop a sense of identity, control impulses, learn cultural language symbols and values, and lay the foundation for developing meaning and a religious perspective on life. Through the child's interaction with the family system, the child develops a sense of self and trust of the environment, as well as developing social roles. When the quality of relationships and interaction in the family is caring and stable, the child can grow and develop without unusual and abnormal problems. However, poor relationships and interaction within the family will prevent the child from growing and making an adequate adjustment to reality. Therefore, facilitating adequate interaction and care within families is very important in the Christian understanding of families and has implications for pastoral counseling.

Another assumption is that the quality of relationships

within the family lessens the influence of technology on the family. Caring relationships help people make sense out of inner and outer experiences in order to get a grip or handle on reality. The crucial issue for the individual is to find adequate symbolic labels in his or her environment that will permit that person to make sense out of reality. The quality of relationships within the family will influence the child's ability to find adequate symbolic objects to label experience. Finding these objects is crucial when one of the first results of the impact of technology is the destruction of symbols adequate for making life meaningful.

When adequate external symbols do not exist that make life meaningful, individuals turn inward to find such symbols. We need to preserve, as much as possible, the quality of symbols outside the person, so that the internal world is not overtaxed. Therefore, one function of pastoral counseling will be to help families improve the quality of relationships so that children will have adequate symbols for dealing with life and for counteracting technological influences. Improving caring relationships in families is one way to preserve the quality of language, which is a conveyor of meaning. More will be said later about language and family relationships.

These four assumptions will be developed with specific reference to the needs of black families and how pastoral counseling with marriage and families from a systems perspective can respond to these needs.

The final assumption is that improving the quality of relationships between generations is crucial in the transmission of values. I indicated in chapter 3 that technology has contributed to lessening the influence of the older generation over the next by helping the nuclear family replace the extended family. When nuclear families replace extended families, many values that help people find meaning in life get lost, and the nuclear family becomes solely responsible for creating new meaning, or doing what Berger calls nomos-building. Pastoral counseling has the function of helping nuclear families construct new meaning when they have very little connection with extended families. When it is possible, pastoral counseling also needs to build counseling models that are multi-generational, assuring the transmission of vital values from one generation to the next.

This section has outlined and examined the theoretical assumptions and foundations of the role of the family in transmitting values. The basic conclusion is that the quality of family relationships relates to the transmission of values and meaning in the family. The pastoral counselor must not only know that family relationships have an impact upon the transmission of values, he or she must also know how to help families develop quality relationships. Family dynamics need to be explored in depth in order to provide a theoretical basis for improving the quality of relationships in families.

THE NEEDS OF BLACK FAMILIES

I have not done a systematic study here on the needs of black families. In fact, very few studies exist that highlight the interactional problems in black families. Robert Staples, in a review of the literature on black families, points out that research has dealt with structural features of the black family, as opposed to interactional processes.[2] Other literature focuses primarily upon psychoanalytic approaches, rather than upon ecological systems perspectives.[3] However, there has been some interest in the relevance of systems theory to the understanding of the dynamics of black families.[4] One theorist who has seriously considered the role of systems theory in families, and black families particularly, is Vincent Foley.[5] His work is based on fifteen years of therapy with black families and lends some light to the needs of black families with regard to family interaction.

One area Foley analyzes is communication patterns. He isolates for consideration incomplete messages, neglect of metacommunication, a need for relabeling, and a neglect of adjectives to describe feelings. These conclusions were based on black families who were in need of marriage or family counseling, and therefore they cannot be generalized to all black families. However, these observations are important to highlight the importance of communication in families in general. All families, regardless of race, have the same communication tasks to perform, and some families do them better than others.

Foley points out that, in incomplete messages, there is a pattern of talking in generalities rather than in specific instances and events. He highlights the need for communication to be concrete and specific, leaving no room for misinterpretation of the message. Specificity, or an attempt to help people communicate in concrete and precise ways, is important to marriage and family therapy with black families.

In my own pastoral counseling it is hard for me to say that the need for specificity is more prevalent among black families than white families. In many instances I have been delightfully surprised at how the relatively uneducated and lower economic level black folks are very concrete and specific when compared to college-trained black folk who have mastered or have become fascinated with abstract thinking. However, studies need to be undertaken that would accurately measure communication patterns in black families with reference to specificity. My intuitive hunch is that speaking with specificity is not related to race or economic status. Specificity of speech seems to be related to personal and family self-esteem as well as to the level of personal autonomy of each family member. This would hold true even in subcultural, colloquial expressions in the black community. Colloquial expressions also have their own degrees of specificity, and they are clear or unclear depending on the people using them. More will be said concerning the relationship between personal autonomy and communication later.

Foley also points out that relabeling is another need in black families. People need help in looking at something in more than one way. This need is not, in my mind, a characteristic of black families alone, but it is a general need or task that families who have poor communication must accomplish. Healthy communicating families will develop patterns that allow them to view things in a variety of ways, both positively and negatively, depending upon the situation, and unhealthy families will tend to have fewer choices in this regard. The issue in the latter case is helping families relabel things, not in negative ways, but in positive ways. This is a helpful technique in family therapy.

Foley also points out that assigning family roles or tasks is crucial to the family's functioning. Economic factors do affect the roles assigned to children by the family. Foley points out that the oldest daughter is often the surrogate parent and is delegated major responsibility, because the parents are busy earning a living. My work with ministers, most of whom were black males, indicates that adult responsibility roles are not just assigned to the oldest female, but to any child willing to perform such a role. When a child is given adult responsibility prematurely, it has a profound influence upon the child's personality. Basically, certain needs related to play as well as to dependency are ignored, and thus become frustrated and exaggerated. These needs for childhood play and dependency do not disappear, but increase in energy and persist into adult life, often causing embarrassment to the person. Beyond this, being given early adult responsibility as a child frequently influences the selection of a mate and choice of a profession for many of the black seminary students I encounter. For many persons in ministry, the childhood role assignment is reenacted in ministry and becomes a real drawback to meeting deep personal needs.

Family boundaries also have emerged as important in Foley's study and in a study carried out by Salvador Minuchin.[6] My own family ministry has also highlighted the need for the maintenance of boundaries or lines of demarcation between parents and children and between generations.[7] Thus, helping to maintain firm but flexible lines between generations and between children and parents is an important function of pastoral counseling.

The final need is for the black male to have the instrumental role as the head of the house, decisionmaker, and breadwinner. My own experience in marriage counseling is that many black males are very sensitive to what they feel is their place in the family, and they desire to be at the head and center of the family as a strong figure.[8] The desire of the black male to be the head of the family (or at least what he understands leadership to mean) has caused many marital conflicts and precipated many resentments and bitter feelings between spouses. How roles are developed and negotiated within black families is very significant to pastoral counseling.

In the next section, a foundation will be laid for understanding the dynamics of some of the needs outlined in this section. Emphasis will be placed upon the central importance of developing self-esteem as the basis for building adequate communication, securing stable family boundaries, and negotiating roles. This foundational material is essential for getting a glimpse into how the family functions and into the processes that undergird the transmission of values.

FAMILY THEORY AND DYNAMICS

The Family as a System

Family here refers to the husband wife and parent child/children relationship that is often called the nuclear family. While the focus will be primarily on the nuclear family, the extended family or the multi-generational family and the one-parent family are also considered to be definitions of the family. I will confine my discussion to the nuclear family in order to make the understanding of family dynamics manageable. However, I will also attempt to build a theoretical link between the nuclear family and the multi-generational family.

Unlike the individualistic approach in some therapeutic methods, systems theory treats the whole family. Within the systems framework, families are viewed as complex entities comprised of a variety of patterns and functions. As a functional unit, the family exists to satisfy some very basic human needs. The family's purposes are to satisfy the individual's need for love and affection, for sex and procreation, and for the rearing and guiding of children. These functions are carried out by specific structural patterns in the family.

In order to carry out its functions, the family operates through transactional patterns that are repetitious, and these patterns establish how, when, and with whom a member relates. According to Salvador Minuchin, these patterns are maintained by explicit and implicit family rules and expectations, and they help the family carry out its functions.[9]

While the family is treated in systems theory rather than the individual, the impact of the family on the individual is given much attention, particularly by Virginia Satir and Murray Bowen. Virginia Satir points out how self-esteem—how one feels about oneself—relates to one's ability to communicate and to accept others as different from oneself.[10] Bowen complements Satir's understanding of self-esteem by linking self-esteem to developing a sense of self apart from the family in which one was reared, and apart from other people. A brief examination of the interrelationships between Satir and Bowen will help shed light on how personal growth and family system functioning relate.[11]

The basic assumption here is that functioning families with well-developed transactional and interactional patterns are composed of adults who are autonomous and differentiated people. It is further assumed that the differentiation of the adults facilitates adequate communication, transactional patterns, roles, and parenting, while undifferentiated adults produce the opposite effects. Here the adults in the family are seen as the prime movers within the family.

Although the family is a system, and is the focus of therapy in many systems-approaches to treatment, the self-esteem of each family member is important. This self-esteem is related to autonomy.

In family systems theory, families begin with a marital dyad, or the married couple. When a child is born into this relationship, the family becomes three, or a triad. When two persons make up a dyad, they must find their identity by achieving a sense of separateness from each other. Simultaneously, the individual must also develop a sense of "we-ness" or togetherness with the others. This process is called the differentiation and communion process. In the marriage bond, the two become one; however, each individual must have a real sense of self as a separate person from the other, so that the marital relationship can facilitate mutual growth. Similarly, the child must also learn who he or she is as a separate person, as well as a family member.

In the process of differentiation, the child has to separate himself or herself gradually from what Bowen calls the family ego-mass. *Ego-mass* here refers to the sense of "we-ness" and togetherness in a family. Initially, the child is unable to differentiate the self from others. However, as the child grows, it will slowly move toward a sense of "I" separate from the family ego-mass. To mature, the child must learn to become an "I" along with being part of a "we."

The family can assist the movement of the child toward a differentiated "I" or an autonomous "I." If the parents are differentiated and autonomous persons, they are in a better position to assist the child through their interaction as parents and as husband and wife. Differentiated parents communicate clearly, maintain proper boundaries between themselves and the child, respond to the child according to the child's developmental needs, and discipline the child with firmness and fairness. Given this interactional environment, the child has a foundation to rely on when moving toward autonomy. Conversely, in families with undifferentiated parents, the child has no environmental foundation to rely on when moving toward differentiation. As a result, the child will find himself or herself stuck together with the parents in an undifferentiated ego-mass.

Self-esteem is related to the level of differentiation that one has achieved from one's original family. In families where there are differentiated adults, children grow up with a good sense of self and a feeling of being worthwhile. The child feels unique and important because his or her needs are not ignored, and feels a sense of separateness from others. Conversely, people in undifferentiated families feel very bad about themselves, and this feeling of low self-worth manifests itself in the inability of the undifferentiated family members to let others be themselves, unique individuals. Everyone must be the same; there is no tolerance for individual differences, and efforts are made to prevent others from leaving the family ego-mass. In these undifferentiated families, members are viewed as extensions of other members and as possessions to be held onto for the personal security of other family members. In these families, the marital conflict is generally severe, and the systems' functioning is inadequate.

Autonomy, or differentiation, is not total separation from the family in the sense of physical and emotional distance. Physical separation is not autonomy, nor is breaking off communication with one's original family. In fact, maintaining intergenerational links is essential in establishing a sense of self. Having roots is as important to one's identity as being autonomous is. It is important to develop a sense of self while one is related to one's parents. Thus distancing does not lead to autonomy, but reinforces nondifferentiation.

Nondifferentiation and Communication

Communication begins soon after the child is born, and the initial foundation for communication is the relationship that exists between the child and the primary nurturing parents. If the primary nurturing parents feel secure about themselves and their relationship, this feeling will be communicated to the child. This enables the child to feel good about himself or herself and frees the child to explore the self and the world with security.

The primary nurturing relationship between the parents and the child is significant for the child's development of communication skills. The child has his or her own private language as an infant, and when he or she begins to grow, develops the facility to internalize external language symbols, which become the foundation of learning shared language symbols of culture. Shared language symbols become the means by which the child learns to orient himself or herself to the world and to find meaning symbols to label experiences. However, if the quality of the relationship between the primary nurturing parents and the child is inadequate, it becomes very difficult for the child to move from his or her private language to a shared language. As a result, a child may not develop the necessary language skills to make an appropriate adjustment to reality. This has often led to early childhood autism—the child's withdrawal from social interaction and failure to learn language tools.

Assuming that the quality of the relationship between the primary nurturing parents and the child is good enough, the child then matures in his or her ability to internalize a shared cultural language. With the increase of the child's capacity for learning and utilizing language symbols, the parental communication skills become very important. If the parents are able to send messages that are clear in content as well as in nonverbal body language and feeling tone, then the child will correspondingly learn to send clear messages. The ability to send clear messages whose verbal content and nonverbal cues and feeling tones are consistent is called *congruence* by Virginia Satir.[12] However, if there is conflict between the actual content, nonverbal cues, and feeling tones, the message is *incongruent*. For the child to develop adequate communication skills there must be congruent communication patterns between parents.

The ability to receive messages is as crucial as the ability to send messages. Chances are that if parents send conflicting messages, they also will have difficulty receiving messages. When there are communication problems, people often filter the message in ways that prevent them from hearing the actual content of the message. One way the sent message is distorted by the hearer is called *relational distortion* in hearing, in which one filters the message in terms of one's relationship with the sender. The receiver hears only that which is consistent with his or her relationship with the sender. If the receiver feels inferior or superior to the sender, the receiver will hear what is sent through the eyes of the inferior or superior position she or he feels that he or she has in that particular relationship. According to Minuchin, the ability to hear clearly requires the person to differentiate between the content of the messages sent, and the relationship-filtering that is based on the interaction of the sender and receiver.[13] This differentiation facility is learned by the child through interaction with parents who send and receive clear messages.

Communication consists of sending and receiving messages. The functional sender sends clear messages that are congruent, and he or she seeks confirmation from the receiver about whether or not the message was received accurately. The dysfunctional sender sends incongruent messages and does not stop to check whether the messages were received accurately. The functional receiver makes sure he or she has really heard the message, and seeks constant feedback; however, the dysfunctional receiver will usually agree or disagree without being clear about the message.

Significant here is the relationship between functional communication, differentiation from the family, and self-esteem. The more one is differentiated from one's family of origin, has a sense of self as separate from others, and feels worthwhile, the more one will be able to send and receive messages clearly. The converse is true also. There is a correlation between lack of differentiation from the family of origin and low self-esteem with dysfunctional communication. The "why" of this correlation has to do with the risk factor. The autonomous person with good self-esteem can risk more of himself or herself because she or he has inner security; whereas the undifferentiated low self-esteem person needs to distort communication in order to control the world around him or her because of her or his inner insecurity.

Affective Styles of Relating and Differentiation

Closely related to the process of communication are affective styles of relating. Affective styles have to do with the way feeling is communicated. In families whose adults have a high degree of differentiation, there is a wide range of levels of communication of feeling. In these families, tender feelings are demonstrated as well as angry feelings; moreover, there is a nurturant style of affection, rather than an aggressive style of affection in these families. *Nurturant* here refers to feelings that contribute to the growth of others as well as oneself. However, aggressive displays of feelings are shown only in the interest of self-preservation and not for the survival of other family members.

In families whose adults are nondifferentiated, with low self-esteem, tender feelings are rarely shared. Violent and angry feelings seem to be the primary level of relating. Moreover, aggressive styles of relating are more prevalent than nurturant sharing. In families that are stuck together or nondifferentiated, it is very difficult for them to break this pattern through their own efforts.

Differentiation and Roles

The roles of family members are largely influenced by the level of differentiation and self-esteem of the adult family members. According to Nathan Ackerman, a *role* is an adaptational unit of the personality that helps the person relate to others in the family, community, and society.[14] As such, it is the social role, or social dimension of the self, or social identity. It has a function similar to that of language in that it helps individuals locate themselves within the family and society. Therefore, as a person develops language skills, he or she also becomes more aware of societal role expectations.

One does not have only one role in the world. Roles are multiple, and one plays different roles depending on the circumstance and situation. A man may be father, husband, primary nurturer, babysitter, breadwinner, church member, and so forth. The woman can be mother, wife, primary nurturant parent or secondary nurturant parent, breadwinner, and so forth. Usually the person plays one role at a time.

Crucial to understanding modern family roles is a distinction that Ackerman makes between social self and private self. While the social role relates to others' expectations and adjustment to social reality, there is also a private self that has continuity in time and does not change when roles are played. The social self can enhance the inner self, and vice versa. Moreover, one can play certain roles with flexibility if the inner sense of self is secure. In fact, people can perform, in a limited way, conflicting roles if the inner self is well developed. However, the real conflict comes when the inner self and social self are in conflict with each other. According to Ackerman, mature people have very little conflict between their social selves and their private selves; they are well integrated. However, in immature people, private and social selves may be in sharp contrast, and playing certain roles may exact a high price for the individual or private self.

Here again differentiation and self-esteem are related to maturity and immaturity relative to social roles and the inner self. The more differentiated one is from the family of origin and the better one feels about oneself, the more one has the capacity for cohesive integration of the inner self and the social roles. The opposite is true, however, for the undifferentiated and low self-esteem person. There is no flexibility and compatibility between the social role and inner self. In this circumstance the person cannot adjust to social roles according to the changing needs he or she might confront in everyday life.

The key issue in families with regard to roles has to do with the adaptability and flexibility of roles within the family. In families whose adult members are well-differentiated individuals, roles are negotiated mutually; they are flexible and can be changed with the need in changing circumstances. They are also complementary, and one partner does not live at the expense of the other, but each partner contributes to the growth of the spouse. The roles are worked out mutually between two mature adults in the family, and there is sharing at all levels of the relationship. In this kind of family, children learn how to perform a variety of roles as well as how to facilitate the growth of others.

In families whose adult members are not well-differentiated, roles are rigid, and there is no role complementarity. Roles are skewed—they favor one spouse over, or at the expense of, the other. There is no negotiation concerning who plays what role, and certain family members live at the expense of others. There is very little sharing of tasks, and roles are only with difficulty adjusted to changing needs and conditions of the family and the external world. In this kind of family, children learn that others are to be dominated or manipulated in order to get where one wants to go, and the child develops a false sense of what it means to be an adult. No one is fulfilled. Everyone lives and feeds off everyone else in a parasitic manner.

Family Differentiation and Boundaries

The family is made up of subsystems that carry out the functions of the family. There are three major functions, which are (1) to develop mutual and complementary roles and sharing accommodation between husband and wife, (2) to rear and guide the children, and (3) to satisfy the individual family members' need for love and affection. The spouse subsystem exists to help spouses work out a mutual relationship; the parent subsystem exists to help guide the children, and the sibling subsystem exists to help work out relationships with peers.[15]

Important here is whether or not the subsystems are well-differentiated. Each subsystem forms a unit, and boundaries or lines of demarcation exist in order for the subsystems to function without unnecessary intrusions from the outside. For example, the spouse subsystem needs to be protected from destructive and unhealthy intrusions from the inlaws, the children, and friends if it is to perform its functions well. The parent subsystem also needs to keep the lines between the parents and the children clear—there should not be any reversal of roles between the children and the parents. Moreover, the children need to maintain peer relationships without over-protection and interference from the parents. The line or boundaries must be firm, but not rigid. Undifferentiated adults have difficulty maintaining the boundaries. They are either too blurred or too rigid. When there are not lines between the boundaries, or blurred boundaries, this is called an *enmeshed* family pattern. On the other extreme, when the boundaries are too rigid, the pattern is called the *disengaged* pattern. Non-differentiated adults will form families whose boundaries are either enmeshed or disengaged, while differentiated adults will form clear and firm, but flexible, boundaries between subsystems. The result of failure to maintain boundaries is that the needs of the family and its members cannot be fulfilled.

Boundaries between generations need to be firm also, but this does not mean that relationships should be cut off. Every family within the extended family has its own integrity, and this integrity is strengthened by the maintenance of boundaries. However, within the boundary maintenance there could be mutual cooperation and nurture of all family members. Beyond this, there does not have to be physical distance between the generations to maintain the boundaries. Differentiated adults of many generations can live in the same household and maintain boundaries that are firm and respected by all.

IMPLICATIONS FOR PASTORAL COUNSELING WITH BLACK FAMILIES

Marriage and family counseling from a systems perspective seeks to bring the resources of the family to bear on marital and family difficulties, rather than focusing on the individual. Therefore, problems such as lack of differentiation and low self-esteem are addressed by an attempt to change the family's transactional patterns, styles, and communication patterns. A pastoral counselor of black families could help the family learn to send and receive clear messages, experiment with different affective styles, develop role complementarity, and firm up boundaries. The methods for accomplishing these tasks are many, but they depend on the needs of the family and the skills training and level of differentiation the counselor has achieved by differentiating from his or her own family of origin. This differentiation, along with supervision, is a very helpful approach to learning family system therapy. More will be said concerning differentiation from the family of origin in the next chapter.

IMPLICATIONS FOR VALUE FORMATION

When communication, roles, boundaries, and styles of relating are well developed and differentiated, they assist the family in the nomos-building task. The stage is set for the transmission of old values and for the creation of new ones. Moreover, family differentiation is transmitted from one generation to the next by the interaction patterns learned in the family of origin. Intervening in the not-so-well-differentiated family in order to assist in differentiation of family patterns and roles will have an important impact on generations to come if the intervention is successful. With successful intervention the way is also clear for the transmission of meaning and values.

There needs to be contact between generations to insure the mutual reinforcement of learned patterns. Families without roots in past generations are cut off from important lessons that contemporary families need in order to respond to present issues. Even nondifferentiated families of the past generations have a great deal to offer and transmit if they have help maintaining boundaries between generations. Intergenerational counseling and ministries are important for insuring the continuity of values.

Finally, religious and societal values are implied in the way the family carries out its tasks. The dignity and worth of persons, the importance of caring relationships, priority goal setting, and examples of grace are all involved in how a family accomplishes its task. Therefore, the process of pastoral counseling with families helps individual members to discover and to clarify their value commitments.

CHAPTER 7

An Approach to Marriage and Family Counseling

The subject of this chapter is the person of the pastor as a marriage and family counselor. Carl G. Jung believed that people intuitively pick up on how the counselor solves his or her problems even when the counselor does not intend this to happen. There is indeed a depth level of communication taking place between pastoral counselor and client that transcends verbal levels. Because of this, the personality of the pastoral counselor cannot be ignored in the process of developing counseling skills. The personal growth and maturity of the pastoral counselor is communicated to the client. Consequently, how well the pastoral counselor has differentiated himself or herself from the family of origin is crucial to the whole counseling process.

Focusing on how the pastoral counselor differentiated himself or herself from the family of origin is crucial for those who will engage in any form of counseling, particularly marriage and family counseling. One must have one's own values and inner strength, rather than cater to, or look for approval from, other people. This assumes that the pastoral counselor is an individuated, differentiated, autonomous person who has established an identity apart from the family of origin, while building a healthy contact and relationship with the family of origin and other people. A well-differentiated pastor is also able to assist others in their own identity issues as they pursue self-differentiation. A well-differentiated pastoral counselor is in a better position to be flexible and spontaneous in the use of his or her person as well as therapeutic resources that need to be brought to bear on the problems that families and marriages present. Therefore, the essential ingredient of marriage and family counseling is the person of the pastoral counselor.

The pastoral-counselor-as-person-approach to the preparation, doing, and learning of marriage and family counseling recognizes that there is no one approach to helping families with their problems. It recognizes that each approach—whether Rogerian, psychoanalytic, behavioral, or rational-emotion systems; or many years of trial and error, supervision, and reflection—has some validity. One must develop the capacity to integrate and organize one's own approach to counseling, and one's unique way of aiding growth in clients emerges as one interacts with clients, peers, and supervisors with increasing competence and facility. Thus, focusing on one's own differentiation process is an important dimension to developing one's own approach to counseling married couples and families.

It can be added that in the counselor-focusing approach, supervision does not imply tampering with one's personal style through conforming to someone else's style. Rather, it means developing one's own person and style through focusing on one's style of interaction with others with the help of others more experienced in the art of counseling. The supervision helps the counselor bring his or her style of interacting into line with the needs and problems of the marriage partners and/or family.

Part of the counselor-focusing process is the centering principle. This principle involves having one's grounding in the Eternal so that one's total identity has a basis within and yet beyond. This is crucial because spiritual resources from beyond the pastoral counselor are made available through the person of the pastoral counselor. It must be added that spiritual resources are not confined to the personal channel alone, however. They are, indeed, made manifest through many other means. But these resources are often made available through the love and concern of the pastoral counselor.

Since there is *no* one approach to counseling, it is very difficult to write a "how to do it" book for the pastoral counselor. Students often come with the expectation that all they need are the right skills and techniques and they would have the necessary tools to do counseling. They soon become frustrated when they begin to take courses in the field of pastoral care and discover that the emphasis is on personal growth and self-discovery as well as on learning skills. Resistance is often stiff when they are urged to discover their own wounds, hurts, and feelings as the source and foundation of their unique approaches to caring for others. It is very difficult to communicate that the real skill in counseling and therapy begins with who one is and how well one has handled what has happened in one's own life. Students rebel when they are told that their own life experiences are the most important reservoir for learning counseling skills and techniques.

The being of the pastoral counselor is the emphasis more than the doing of the therapy. Here, *being* refers to the living existence of the pastoral counselor; therefore, the pastoral counselor works toward being the living embodiment of the facilitative dimension of caring. *Doing,* on the other hand, refers to putting into effect or carrying to completion the task of counseling. Being is that foundation of doing, and doing without being is empty, hollow, and ineffectual. Therefore, the emphasis here is on the student's personal growth, in recognition that facilitative skills will emerge from this growth.

This chapter, therefore, will not teach how to do marriage and family counseling. It will instead deal with the being of the pastoral counselor in terms of self-actualization and how this can be translated into facilitative skill development. It is important for the prospective pastoral counselor to undergo and to accomplish self-actualization with some degree of success as a prerequisite of developing skill. It has been shown empirically that client growth is related to the personal growth of the counselor.[1] The focus here is therefore on the personal growth of the pastoral counselor, particularly self-actualization and differentiation from one's family of origin. Personal differentiation from one's family of origin is fundamental to learning marriage and family therapy, and is also fundamental in helping the prospective counselor to *be* what he or she expects to accomplish with others in marriage and family counseling. This approach is based on my personal observation that many of the individual, marital, and family problems that I treat have their origin in the families in which these people were reared. This is true of so-called normal individuals, marriages, and families, as well as of troubled people. Thus, spending time helping the prospective counselor differentiate from the family of origin is necessary prior to the counselor's helping clients and parishioners do the same thing.

THE FOCUSING PRINCIPLE AND BLACKNESS

The focusing principle is consistent with the meaning of blackness defined in the introduction of this work. Black students often have resisted the resources available to them for learning counseling and therapy because they feel that they may lose their uniqueness and spontaneity through the exposure to courses and training developed for whites in white institutions. The focusing principle seeks to help one discover that uniqueness within, so that it can become the central integrating principle around which one's personal style and therapeutic skills can be organized.

When I was interviewed for acceptance into the Ph.D. program in Pastoral Psychology and Counseling at Boston University, I was informed that the training they had to offer would perhaps be irrelevant to the needs of the black community. However, this limitation having been stated by my interviewers, they invited me to join the program with the challenge that it was my own responsibility to draw from what they offered whatever might be relevant. Beyond this, I was encouraged to do part of my practicum experience in a black setting, so that I would be sure to proceed with the integration of what was relevant into a unique approach. It was from the above urging and experience that I learned the concept of focusing and its importance for my own ministry of pastoral counseling.

GETTING IN TOUCH WITH THE FAMILY OF ORIGIN

Self-actualization begins with the exploration of one's family of origin. The family of origin is the family in which one was born. It includes the significant others within a household who assisted in the rearing of children, whether they were blood-related or not, or whether original parents or extended-family relatives; the significant others who helped us develop our patterns for interacting with the world. Whether one was raised by one's own parents or by relatives or friends, one is born into some interactive family group that greatly influences how one deals with growth and development and relationships with the world.

It is important for the learning of marriage and family counseling to reengage this original family and biographical environment as a source of one's focusing and skills. We are social and historical beings who bring into adult life significant family resources and problems through an unconscious memory process. Reentering this unconscious memory through a variety of means can assist one in further growth and differentiation. This reentering process stimulates insights into one's own patterns and ways of interacting in the present, as well as enabling the learning of important lessons that can be of real assistance in helping others differentiate themselves from their families of origin. Three approaches for reentering the unconscious dimensions of one's childhood family will be examined. These are the family genogram, family sculpting, and the family-of-origin paper.

Family Genogram

The family genogram is a basic method of getting in touch with one's own family of origin. It is tracing one's own family tree and influences back into history. It is getting in touch with the roots of one's personality; therefore, getting in touch with the sources of one's self. Moreover, having a knowledge of, and a cognitive and experiential relationship with, one's generational history is indispensible to a sense of positive identity for the black pastoral counselor.

In the pastoral care department of the Interdenominational Theological Center, we begin training for pastoral counseling and family ministry by helping the student explore his or her autobiographical history as far back as the family's oral history will allow. This is essential for helping the student deepen an awareness of areas of identity, similarity, and dissimilarity with the historical past. This aids the process of identity formation by helping the student to "own and befriend" the similarity, while affirming and enjoying the areas of personality uniqueness. Such a process contributes to the self-understanding of the student as an independent person responsible for how he or she uses life, and at the same time confirms the continuity and constancy with the past.

The genogram is a structural diagram of a generational relationship system.[2] It is an essential model for beginning the process of moving backward into the family's interactional history, into the unconscious memory of family dynamics. It either begins with the older generations and moves forward, or it moves in the other direction, from the recent generations to the older generations. Including the names, ages, the dates of marriages, deaths, births, and divorces, the person can explore important events and crises in the development of his/her own family history. In this process, connections, patterns, and traditions that are the cement holding generations together are revealed. Diagram 1 reflects a chart of an actual genogram structure.

Diagram 1   FAMILY GENOGRAM

This is a family genogram design. It is a four-generation model. As one constructs one's genogram, attention to feelings and nonverbal communication is important. Moreover, this exercise is an excellent method of gathering intake data. For example, it lists ages, deaths, marriages, and other information that will emerge as one begins to construct the genogram.

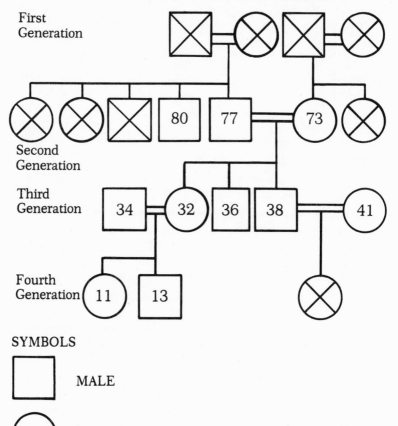

First
Generation

Second
Generation

Third
Generation

Fourth
Generation

SYMBOLS

☐   MALE

◯   FEMALE

✕   DECEASED

＝   MARRIED

Beyond helping the student know and befriend the past as a continuation and differentiation process in identity formation, the genogram exercise is a means of helping the student experience what parishioners and clients will undergo when doing such an exercise themselves. Undergoing this process in training and reflecting upon it are important ways of learning about others.

Family Sculpting

Family sculpting is "an arrangement of people or objects that express [sic] their family relationship to one another" at a particular point in time.[3] It is different from the family genogram in that it is confined to specific periods of the family's life together. It is not generally used to portray intergenerational continuity. It is primarily concerned with structural arrangements of the interaction of family members, and how these structural arrangements reveal family dynamics.

Like the family genogram, the sculpting offers a tool to the pastoral counselor and pastor to enter into his or her own family of origin. The exercise can be done in small groups, in a classroom setting, or in counseling. It is primarily a nonverbal exercise, but talking is an important dimension to add in order to get the most out of the exercise. The value of the verbal dimension is that the sculptor can explore his or her feelings as he or she chooses others or objects to stand in places that represent how the sculptor perceives the family arrangement. Indeed, the sculpting of one's family of origin is accompanied by strong feelings when one relives and experiences joyous as well as painful moments.

It is important to give the theoretical rationale of the family sculpting exercise. This will show how such an action can aid the self-differentiation process.

Family sculpting is a form of art, but it is not a static art like painting. Rather, it is a theoretical creation—the director creates a stage production out of his or her own inner life. Because it is a creation out of the inner life of the sculptor, it has a strong emotional component; it is a vehicle for reexperiencing and recovering lost memories in the unconscious. The kinesthetic, tactile, and visual dimension of the stage production is a symbolic representation of deeply felt feelings and perceived and forgotten events. Thus, family sculpting gives access to one's memory of past family dynamics.

Family sculpting has two phases. The first phase is constructing one's family of origin by placing family members and/or physical objects in places that represent the physical arrangements as perceived by the sculptor (see Family Sculpting, Diagram 2). The second phase is sculpting the family as one ideally wished the family to have been (see Family Sculpting, Diagram 3). This second step is important because it gives one an experience of what it is like to reconstruct one's family the way one would have liked it to be. It imprints upon the mind of the sculptor that one is *not,* ultimately, a passive agent in one's development. Although one cannot actually recreate the family of origin, one can begin to understand that one can create one's present family with the cooperation of the other family members.

As one participates in this exercise, one reconnects with the family of origin in order to experience it anew, to befriend it, and to differentiate from it. One must work through some family differentiation experiences as a prerequisite to being an effective marriage and family counselor.

Next is a diagram of an actual sculpting. This is a view of what a sculpting looks like if viewed from the top. Pay attention to the physical distance.

In Diagram 2 there is a great physical distance between the sculptor and the rest of the family. There is a great distance between the father and mother. However, in the reconstructed ideal family, the distance has narrowed.

Family-of-Origin Paper

The family-of-origin paper is an academic and experiential exercise that helps the pastoral counselor explore in depth

FAMILY SCULPTING

Diagram 2 (Perceived Arrangement)

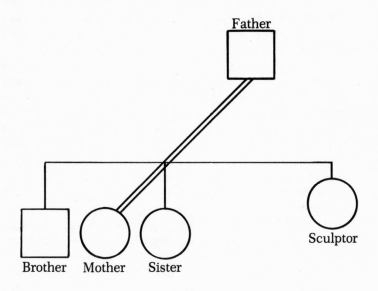

Diagram 3 (Reconstructed)

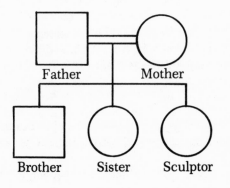

the relationships with significant family members, crises, and events in the life of the family one has grown up in. It is similar to the genogram in that it can be multi-generational, and it is similar to the sculpting in that it explores the family structure. The difference between the family of origin paper and these other exercises is that one explores family relationships in depth over a longer period of time. This method is similar to the uncovering approaches of psychotherapy in that it helps one see connections between one's present development and the family of origin.

Students in my classes often point out that they did not live in a household of their original father and mother. They were reared by relatives and/or surrogate parents. All three of these exercises do not require that one be raised by sanguine or blood parents. In fact, the same family dynamics exist in families whose child-rearers are fictive (surrogate) parents. In other words, these exercises can apply to sanguine and fictive households, and all three have relevance for those who were not raised by blood parents.

The academic dimension is helpful in the family-of-origin paper because it helps the student reflect on family dynamics through the use of theory. It helps the student learn the family dynamics through reflection, and at the same time, grow in insight concerning the influences of her or his family of origin upon her or his present behavior. This theory can open up possibilities for new relationships with family members as well as for contemporary relationships. As a result of this academic and experiential exercise, the student will often see how the family of origin has influenced the choice of a mate, current family interaction patterns, and the choice of a profession. Students often point out that the theoretical exercise helps them gain some objectivity, freedom, and differentiation from childhood family difficulties that they brought to their marriages.

Enough cannot be said about the importance of this exercise for helping the student learn marriage and counseling skills through the process of differentiation from the family of origin. Under the guidance of instructors and coaches (who are usually teachers in pastoral care and Christian education), the students reflect on their own differentiation process to gain academic and experiential expertise.

Family Detriangling

The major rationale for doing a family-of-origin paper is to help the person or student to know who he or she is as a family member as well as to know who he or she is apart from the family members. To be mature adults, we must learn to take the "I position" in relationship to our family of origin, and in learning this, we can help others to do so when we are pastoral counselors. In fact, learning to become a therapist, according to Vincent Foley, is "undergoing the process of working on one's own family system and experiencing the difference between responding and reacting."[4]

Detriangling is learning to become separate from one's family of origin in order that one's identity as an autonomous person be established. Triangling is the process of parents' drawing the child into the parental conflict when there is tension between the spouses. This principle involves more than the parents; it can involve a tension-filled relationship between parent and child or other paired relationship, and the bringing in of a third party who does not have the expertise to help.

When the parents triangle with a child, it usually has a damaging influence on the child. In fact, the child has no experience to help the parents, and the result is that the child is prevented from learning self-actualizing skills. Therapy with adults is often a process of helping them detriangle themselves from the marital difficulties of their parents so that the self-actualization process can continue. In many adults the same dynamics that existed within their family of origin exist in their adult lives, and detriangling offers freedom from these dynamics by enabling the person to respond rather than react to the family of origin.

Reaction is a way of responding to one's family of origin

when one feels there is really no hope for becoming a separate person. One reacts to this hopelessness either through rebellion or through conforming to parental expectations. In either manner of responding one is not free. The ideal is for one to respond to the family of origin in such a way that the direction of one's life comes from within, and not from the expectations of others. This inner direction is a pro-action stance based on one's own sense of self. Detriangling contributes to this inner focusing and helps the person respond without rebellion or conformity.

Since the extended family is so important to the black community, it is necessary for the black person to find ways to be separate and independent without severing ties with the family of origin and other relatives. The concept of detriangling is crucial here, because it posits that no real identity is attained by severing one's relationship with the family of origin and the extended family. Real identity emerges as one develops a sense of self and as one keeps interactional contact with one's biographical history. Physical distancing or emotional distancing do not produce freedom. Rather, they continue a form of bondage. Detriangling and its methods, on the other hand, help the person maintain healthy contact with parents and other relatives, while helping the person to differentiate himself or herself from them.

Detriangling as a concept and method has been developed by Murray Bowen. Bowen introduces his concept by pointing out that the potential counselor must begin to control his or her emotional reactivity to the family of origin, by visiting it as often as possible, and by developing an ability to be a participant observer in it. In these ways the person begins to see how he or she plays an important role in the family's interaction patterns. Once the person recognizes how he or she participates in the family's dynamic patterns, he or she can begin to differentiate himself or herself from the "myths, images, distortions, and triangles of the family of origin." Bowen warns that the detriangling process cannot be accomplished quickly and should be supervised by one who is more experienced in detriangling. He has found this process more effective for the maturing of potential of counselors than actual psychotherapy.

There are three methods of detriangling. These methods are (1) building person-to-person relationships with family members, (2) becoming a better observer and controlling one's emotional reactiveness, and (3) detriangling oneself from emotional situations. These methods will be discussed briefly.

Bowen says the following about person-to-person relationships: "In broad terms, a person to person relationship is one in which two people can relate personally to each other, about each other, without talking about others [triangling], and without talking about 'impersonal things.'"[5]

Such a procedure is extremely difficult and is often resisted by the parents of those trying to detriangle themselves. Yet, if they are successful, the dividends are great. According to Bowen, developing a person-to-person relationship with any member of the family of origin and the extended family makes one grow up faster than anything in his therapeutic experience. However, because many difficulties may emerge, it is good for the detriangling person to have a coach who can assist the person at many critical points.

One difficulty that might emerge is the feeling of guilt engendered by building the person-to-person relationship. For example, one seminary student wanted to be free of her mother's constantly dragging her into her marital problems. Every time the student would call on the phone, her mother would begin to complain about the father's inadequacies. This pattern had been established since she was about eight years old. As she tried to establish a person-to-person relationship and attempted to guide her mother into talking about their relationship as daughter and mother, the mother resisted. This made the daughter feel guilty and depressed, feeling she would never extricate herself from the triangle. Rather than doing insight therapy for the guilt, I coached her by role-playing with her the conversations she had with her mother, so that she could rehearse and gain the confidence to relate to her mother in a different way. She had a lot of ego strength, and was still engaged in the process of detriangling a year later. The last report was that their relationship is more personal than it has ever been.

The second procedure is to become a participating observer while controlling one's own emotional reactivity. Such a process will help one get outside the family emotional system. It is important not to take sides or be drawn into the family arguments. For example, when parents attempt to bring one into their conflict (as in the case in the above paragraph), it is important to find a way—verbally, nonverbally, and behaviorally—not to be manipulated into the parental conflict. However, this cannot be accomplished by physical distancing. The growth comes by maintaining contact with the parents. After thirty-six years of life I have managed to say to my parents, "I ain't getting in that mess." They smile and cease to drag me into it.

My growth came when I realized I had a need to referee for my parents' difficulty. However, I learned that my parents really did not need me to help them with their problems. They had managed to be together for over forty years without my help. When I realized this, it was easier to detriangle myself from them. As one can see, it takes three people to make a triangle. The child has just as much need to be in the triangle as the parents have need for him or her. Thus the child often resists detriangling as much as the parents do.

Detriangling the self from emotional situations is closely related to controlling one's emotional reactivity. The goal in this effort is to maintain contact with the family of origin and the extended family emotional system, without, however, taking sides, without counterattacking, and without defending oneself. In other words, one is called to take a neutral position in relationship to the family's manipulative emotional system. However, one is free to be emotionally spontaneous and have genuine feelings in the person-to-person relationships as long as one is not defensive, taking sides, and counterattacking.

The detriangling process is not without its problems. The basic problem is that the person must give up his or her childhood position in the family. This frightens most of us and temporarily inflicts a loss of identity. There is a transition period between the old identity and the new identity.

It has been pointed out that the family genogram, family sculpting, and the family-of-origin paper contribute to the differentiation process as well as to learning the skills of counseling. This is the case with detriangling also; it is especially true with learning to counsel. Learning not to get caught up in one's own manipulative family emotional system can be generalized to family and marriage counseling as well as to transference-oriented, in-depth counseling. One can learn how to escape the manipulation of the emotional systems of families, marriages, and individuals by detriangling oneself from one's own family of origin and extended family. The basic skill to be learned in supervision is how to escape the emotional system of the clients in order to be of help to them. Detriangling gives one a head start.

PROBLEM SOLVING IN MARRIAGE AND FAMILY COUNSELING

It has been indicated throughout this chapter that differentiation from the family of origin is essential to learning marriage and family counseling. The assumption underlying this way of looking at counseling is that the person of the pastoral counselor is the major therapeutic agent, and method is secondary. Also, adequate self-differentation frees the counselor to select from a variety of counseling methods in order to respond to the presenting problems and needs of the client.

Good self-differentiation frees the pastoral counselor to do problem-solving therapy. Problem-solving therapy is selecting from a variety of counseling methods those methods and procedures that respond to the needs of the clients.[6] One method begins with exploring the nature of the presenting problem, taking a detailed history of the problem, and discovering the social and personal factors influencing the problem. As the data is gathered, the pastoral counselor assesses some of the key dynamics and structures that have the potential to aid or hinder the solution of the presenting problem. Thus it is crucial to have information about the personal histories of each person in the family—generationally if needed—as well as a history of interactions in communication, roles, boundaries, triangles, and self-differentiation.

After a detailed history is taken, the counselor should explore with the clients what they want to do about the problem they present. Once this is done, the counselor can indicate how he or she can help them solve their problem, and indicate precisely what methods will be used to help them with the problem solving. This phase of the counseling is called the *contract phase*.[7]

The problem-solving approach to family counseling is primarily designed to deal with families. However, some aspects of it can be utilized in all forms of therapy. We will confine ourselves to the family for the time being.

In problem-solving therapy the focus is on the family as a corporate unit of interaction. From this perspective, the family is viewed as the problem, rather than the individual member, and the techniques used are usually directed to systemic dimensions; such as patterns of communication, manipulation of boundaries, experimentation with different roles, and learning to behave in different ways. Focusing on systemic dynamics necessitates that the counselor be active rather than passive and focus on current issues rather than on the past. Being a director and educator are within the scope of this corporate model. However, the major contribution of the corporate model is the importance of the counselor as model of what the family members expect to be, particularly in communicating, relating to others with compassion, and treating members of the family in ways that engender self-esteem.

Modeling makes self-differentiation very important. How can the pastoral counselor model something which he or she has not developed in his or her own interactive life? Effective modeling is a result of adequate self-differentiation from the family of origin.

I have deliberately not presented a step-by-step "how to do it" model of family and marriage counseling. I have emphasized the personality development of the pastoral counselor. This is a basic necessity before adopting a problem-solving approach or any approach to counseling. Thus, the pastoral counselor needs to engage in the self-differentiation process initially, and then pick and choose methods and skills related to concrete presenting problems of clients. Only in this way can the pastoral counselor retain some uniqueness.

Uniqueness is crucial to the black pastoral counselor in supervision training. One must learn who one is and learn counseling skills by plunging into one's own family of origin. This presents a unique opportunity for black pastoral counselors to hold on to and enrich their unique history. Through the process of befriending and differentiating from this history, one is ready to model, under supervision, in the marriage and family counseling process.

Part of the emphasis in this chapter has been upon the corporate model of family and marriage counseling. I am not limiting myself to this orientation alone since I follow the presenting problem approach. Therefore, I also utilize one-to-one psychoanalytic approaches as well as systems and behavioral approaches to marriage counseling. The psychoanalytic methods will be the subject of later chapters.

PART III

Depth Pastoral Counseling and Spiritual Values

CHAPTER 8

Nurturing Images and Depth Pastoral Counseling

The value transmission in pastoral care and counseling can be assisted by the use of symbols and images that appear in the dreams of black people. As indicated in chapter 1, images historically played an important role in the life of black people, and their use in pastoral counseling can reinforce the values emerging from the black Christian experience.

Images appearing in dreams are often archetypal resources for manifesting collective history, and these archetypes often embody value resources for personal growth. These value resources frequently form an important link with the historical continuity and primordial Source of eternal values, which undergird and buttress the values emerging from the mediating structures of the family and the church. Access to these values is not only through these mediating structures, but also is available to each individual, through archetypes manifesting themselves through the collective unconscious. These two dimensions, the mediating structure and the personal collective unconscious, can work together and reinforce each other.

How dream images can be explored for their significance to personal growth is basically a contribution of psychoanalysis. The work of Jung, which has already been outlined, has

137

been especially helpful to me in using images in depth pastoral counseling with black clients. This chapter and the following chapter are attempts to illustrate how depth pastoral counseling can use dream image exploration and interpretation to assist in the reaffirmation of important cultural and spiritual values in people's daily lives. These values are the affirmation of the inherent worth of each person, the importance of the growth of the self, the significance of relationships with others and God in the growth process, and the power of God working through the unconscious and other people to facilitate growth.

Because there is a shift now from the mediating structure and nomos-building model of the transmission of values to a more intrapersonal and interpersonal orientation of depth pastoral counseling, it is necessary to give some rationale for the place of a one-to-one model of pastoral counseling in a corporate context. Pastoral counseling is of no value if it is cut off from the Source of values and the caring community of believers. In fact, pastoral counseling should be done in a context of a Christian caring community like the local church and exist as an extension of its ministry. In this way, pastoral counseling takes on a deeper meaning, as Don S. Browning defines in *The Moral Context of Pastoral Care*. If pastoral counseling is part of a community context, people are already part of a symbolic and spiritual world-view that informs and gives perspective to pastoral counseling.[1] Pastoral counseling in the context of the local church and similar institutions is consistent with the corporate understanding of pastoral care in the black church. In fact, it enhances the corporate ministry of the local church, rather than detracts from it.

THE MEANING OF DEPTH PASTORAL COUNSELING

The depth pastoral counseling explored here is a long-term counseling relationship between a pastoral counselor and a client that uses their interaction to free the client's internal resources for growth. A warm, trusting, and empathetic relationship between the pastoral counselor and client is necessary for the emergence and use of nurturing images that strengthen and support spiritual and community values. This warm relationship generally consists of empathy, respect, concreteness, genuineness, and immediacy. Moreover, the depth pastoral counseling methods discussed here will include the skillful use of transference and counter-transference, dream interpretation, and process and interaction interpretation. The first section of this chapter will examine the assumptions underlying nurturing image theory, the second will elaborate on the core characteristics of pastoral counseling and the skills mentioned above. The third section will illustrate the use of images in the depth pastoral counseling approach with a case study.

Nurturing Images

Values and tradition are available through images. As Fromm and Jung have pointed out, people have access to eternal values that have continuity in time through turning inward (see chapter 2, pp. 52 and 53). However, turning inward to find a source of values and the turning inward associated with emotional difficulties through regression are different processes, and they need to be distinguished.[2] Regression is involved in both processes, but the regression associated with emotional difficulties produces dynamics that are infantile, associated with forgotten wants and needs that were frustrated in childhood. On the other hand, numinous dreams and images move beyond the process of childhood fixation in regression and produce images that signal a shift in emotional life toward positive growth. Thus, moving inward and finding eternal meaning and nurturing images, the person has overcome the emotional conflict to the extent that it does not dominate the search for meaning. The emotional conflict has been moved from the dominant role it plays. This allows the client to proceed to the value dimensions and nurturing images that are part of his or her collective unconscious and have their foundation outside the individual. Such nurturing images are considered manifestations of the ground of being in which the person stands.

I am suggesting, as Jung does, that there is more to the unconscious than emotional conflicts; there is, indeed, a vast reservoir of value, tradition, and meaning within the unconscious that has its basis in objective, external reality, and is available through images from the collective unconscious. In this context, the internal life of the individual and caring relationships with others become vehicles of this objective meaning. Therefore, depth pastoral counseling can be seen as an opportunity, not only to help people resolve deep emotional conflicts caused by the problems of life, but also to help them get in touch with sources of eternal tradition within themselves that are made available through images.

Moving the person beyond emotional problems to nurturing images requires in many cases the skills of a psychoanalytic oriented psychotherapist.[3] A warm relationship is essential for one to really have access to one's nurturing inner life. In fact, the warm caring relationship employed in psychotherapy not only facilitates the emergence of nurturing images; it also helps people to actualize the implication of the experience of the image in everyday life. The skills of psychoanalytic therapy are needed to assist in the resolution of the emotional conflict and to assist in the emergence of nurture images, as well as to concretize the implications of the experience of the images.

Nurturing images are concrete forms through which eternal sources and resources from beyond the person are made available to the person. According to Jung, these forms, or archetypes, are often numinous, and encountering them has the power to integrate one's life in a way similar to the integration that occurs in religious conversion (see chapter 3). However, one warning must be added here. The images occurring primarily in dreams and in semidream states are not always numinous or nurturing; they can have multiple meanings, and even be irrational and pathological.[4] Yet nurturing images do appear and present signs for potential growth and the resolution of significant emotional problems.

The Dimensions of Pastoral Counseling

In chapter 1, the concepts of empathy, respect, genuineness, and concreteness were defined. This section will summarize the definitions of these terms and include a discussion of immediacy.

The most essential step in long-term pastoral counseling is to build a relationship of trust and respect with the client. In this sense, long-term pastoral counseling is no different from any other counseling relationship. However, when pastoral counseling goes beyond the two- to three-week time period and involves an agreement between the pastoral counselor and the client to work on certain goals involving personality growth and change, long-term or in-depth pastoral counseling is in its beginning stages.[5]

Core Dimensions of Pastoral Counseling

In any form of pastoral counseling, as well as in the beginning stages of long-term pastoral counseling, empathy, respect, genuineness, and concreteness are the chief ingredients of the pastoral counseling relationship. It is crucial for the pastoral counselor to relate to the client on a feeling level, and this is done by making an effort to tune in to the client's wavelength. The crucial element in this form of empathy has been outlined by Robert R. Carkhuff and Bernard Berenson:

> The therapist's ability to communicate at high levels of empathic understanding appears to involve the therapist's ability to allow himself to experience or merge in experience of the client, reflect upon this experience while suspending his own judgements, tolerating his own anxiety, and communicating this understanding to the client.[6]

The therapist can communicate this empathy by being fully human himself or herself and not giving purely mechanical responses and only intellectual understanding. Empathy is not a technique or an academic skill, but is an experiential quality developed as one learns to be one's genuine self.

Closely related to being fully oneself is the respect or regard that one has for oneself. One cannot "respect the feelings and experiences of others" if one "cannot respect his own feelings and experiences."[7] Communicating respect for the client is done with understanding and warmth. It is through the counselor's effort to understand and to be warm that the client perceives respect and empathy.

The growth of the pastoral counselor in being oneself as well as in respecting and accepting one's own feelings and experiences is also important in being genuine with the client. A pastoral counselor can establish a therapeutic relationship with the client to the degree to which he or she can be honest with himself or herself and with the client. This does not mean that the counselor is irresponsible with genuine feelings that are negative or positive. But it means that the pastoral counselor "makes an effort to employ" his or her "responses constructively as a basis for further inquiry" into their relationship. The focus is always on the needs of the client when one is sharing genuine feelings.

Concreteness is very important for therapist and client alike. It involves the direct expression of specific feelings and experiences, even when there is emotional content.[8] This helps the feelings become part of the therapeutic interaction. It is also essential in counseling when feelings are the key to corrective emotional growth and maturity. The problems of long-term therapy frequently involve defending against the emergence of strong feelings, particularly negative feelings. Hence concreteness in the context of a warm, understanding relationship is very important. However, as will be indicated later under the topic of transference, there are limits to how concrete the pastoral counselor needs to be about his or her personal life.

These four ingredients are crucial in the earlier stages of counseling, whether brief or long-term. However, as the counseling proceeds, the quality of the interaction between the pastoral counselor and the client changes. It becomes more intense, and the longer the relationship lasts, the more the client will begin to react to the pastoral counselor in terms of the inner emotional conflict. The longer the pastoral counseling relationship lasts, the more the client will externalize the internal emotional conflict, and the counseling relationship takes on the contours of the inner imaginary life of the client.

In this context of long-term pastoral counseling where the internal imaginary life of the client is projected into the counseling relationship, immediacy becomes very important. Immediacy refers to the nature of the relationship between the pastoral counselor and client in the actual sessions. For example, in brief pastoral counseling, the immediacy involves the warmth and understanding of the pastoral counselor and the client's response to it. However, as the long-term relationship begins in pastoral counseling, the warmth, genuineness, concreteness, and understanding facilitate the emergence of the inner emotional life of the client, and this changes the nature of the relationship; thus, the nature of immediacy changes. It changes from a more reality-based immediacy to a more fantasized immediacy in the client's mind.

The significance of immediacy is that in pastoral counseling, especially, the pastoral counselor needs to help the client talk about what is taking place in the interaction with the pastoral counselor. Facilitative immediacy requires the pastoral counselor to handle a depth of closeness in the interpersonal counseling relationship as well as the feelings associated with such closeness. Here again, the ability of the pastoral counselor to be at home with his or her own feelings as well as the feelings of the client is crucial.

This brings us to the themes of transference and countertransference. When the client begins to project onto the pastoral counselor his or her inner imaginary life, transference takes place. The client begins to treat the pastoral counselor "as if" he or she were a significant other from the client's past. From an object-relations theoretical perspective, transference is the client's responding to the pastoral counselor as if he or she were an internalized object from the client's inner life. By doing this transference, the client is transforming the counseling relationship into a fantasized replica of his or her imaginary internal life.

Countertransference refers to how the pastoral counselor responds to the transference of the client. It usually takes two forms. It can often stimulate the unresolved conflicts of the pastoral counselor, which can easily overshadow the client's needs and issues. Or it can stimulate the pastoral counselor to respond by gratifying the transference needs of the client. This is usually done by conforming to the transference expectation of client. Gratifying the transference needs of the client only intensifies the imaginary distortion of the counseling relationship and is not helpful to the client's growth.

Handling the transference without gratifying the transference needs of the client requires a great deal of maturity and skill developed under many years of supervision. The same is true for the pastoral counselor's inner conflicts that remain unresolved. In the latter case one's own psychotherapy, under supervision, is crucial.

In supervised psychoanalytic-oriented psychotherapy, there are two ways I have found comfortable to deal with the transference distortion. Both ways involve the use of immediacy. The first is encouraging the client to talk about feelings and attitudes toward me in the immediate session, for the purpose of exploration only. Here the emphasis is, not on insight, but upon helping the client feel comfortable with having, and talking with me about, those feelings. Then, when I think the client is ready, I interpret the feeling in the light of transference distortion. I help the client see the similarity between our relationship and those with significant others in his or her past.

These two techniques are called "working through the transference distortion." The first stage of working through the transference distortion is helping the client deal with the immediate counseling relationship without interpretation. The second step is interpreting the true nature of the transference distortion. The purpose of this latter step is to help the client grow emotionally by making distinctions between the distorted transference counseling relationship and the real counseling relationship.

Another method associated with immediacy is the pastoral counselor's use of self. Here the counselor observes his or her own feelings generated in the counseling relationship and uses these feelings constructively for the benefit of the client. This is related to the concept of genuineness mentioned earlier. However, here the feelings are generated in a distorted transference relationship, whereas the use of genuineness is more related to less distorted transference relationship.

Timing is very important in the use of one's own feelings, and their use depends upon whether the client is in the first or second stage of working through transference. In either case, the counselor's own feelings are communicated to the client in a way that facilitates the client's exploration of his or her own feelings. The inappropriate use of self by the pastoral counselor may take the focus away from the client and put it upon the pastoral counselor. This should be avoided.

Self-disclosure should be limited in long-term psychoanalytically oriented psychotherapy. Premature self-disclosures will often interfere with the development of the transference distortion. However, self-disclosure and self-revelation by the pastoral counselor is very appropriate after the transference distortion has developed and has been worked through, and the counseling is in the termination phase. At this stage, the client has worked through the distortion sufficiently to accept the realness of his or her pastoral counselor.

It must be added that the pastoral counselor's self-disclosure is only inappropriate when doing extensive psychoanalytic "uncovering" psychotherapy,[9] which deals with personality change and working through character defenses. However, in psychotherapy, which is not extensive and is focused on immediate problem-solving issues, self-disclosure is an essential and desirable method of pastoral counseling.

Dream images can appear at any state of pastoral counseling and can be utilized in a variety of ways. Here the goal is to understand how the nurturing image might be utilized in pastoral counseling.

Exploring Images

Nurturing images and numinous images are available to people, especially through dreams. The eternal resources, which are part of objective reality, are often available through the collective unconscious, which is the reservoir of social, historical, and ontological truths accumulated since the beginning of humanity.

The emphasis on the numinous-transforming-nurturing-function dimension of dreams is not intended to suggest that all dreams must be so. Dreams have a variety of meanings and interpretations, and an interpreter of dreams must take his or her direction for interpretation from the person experiencing the dream. Dreams have a variety of functions, which include "ineluctable truths, philosophical pronouncements, illusions, wild fantasies, memories, plans, anticipations, irrational experiences, even telepathic visions."[10]

Dreams can also be used for a variety of purposes by the pastoral counselor. They can be used diagnostically to discuss the emotional and spiritual condition of the client. They can be used at any stage of the counseling process and in any form of counseling. They can be utilized to understand the nature of transference resistance and transference compliance,[11] as well as in working through the transference. Dream images and dream interpretation can be used to help the client discover different dimensions of the self that need to be integrated into a whole personality.

Certain methods of image exploration have been helpful to me. The first method is to attempt to understand the waking events immediately surrounding the dream. The second method is to have the person explore the various meanings that the dreamer sees in the dream. Third, the dreamer is asked by free-association, to identify each image in the dream as a living or non-living entity. Free association is a method whereby the person focuses on the image and reports, uncensored, whatever first comes to his or her mind. Fourth, the person may be asked to identify with the images, objects, and personages as if they were the dreamer. The dreamer is asked to speak in the first person and to indicate what he or she is doing as part of the dream. Over a period of time a pattern begins to emerge and the meaning becomes apparent. The actual revelation of the meaning of the dream could take one session or many sessions.

Numinous images may appear long before the person is ready to accept their full impact. In fact, resistance to the implications of the images may force the person to resist any hint that it might have transforming qualities.

The counselor's interpretations of the image must be given when the dreamer is ready to accept them. Jung points out that the dreamer must grow up to the truth of the dream.[12] Therefore, the pastoral counselor may be aware of some of the dream elements before the dreamer is, but these insights must be stored in the counselor's memory bank until the timing is right. How to determine this requires skill, experience, and training, and cannot be easily communicated on paper. However, it is easier to tell in retrospect that an interpretation is premature, particularly when the interpretation does not facilitate the dreamer's exploration of the dream.

Image exploration is a therapeutic art. Although there may be numinous qualities to the dream, this is no excuse to ignore what modern science, particularly psychoanalysis, has to say about the methods of interpreting dreams. While one may not subscribe to the psychoanalytic perspective for understanding the dream, psychoanalytic insight concerning people's readiness to accept interpretations needs to be taken very seriously.

CASE ILLUSTRATION

This case illustration comes from my teaching and counseling. I see the seminary as an extension of the church, sharing in its liberation ministry. Moreover, the seminary is a caring Christian community and the classroom is a microcosm where the principles of faith and care are explored and practiced. Thus, this case is constructed with the background of a caring community in mind. I view my counseling as an extension of the ministry of the church, rather than as a private practice.

Roland is a black male who was 25 years old at the time of his counseling. He had grown up in a rural Southern town and had graduated from seminary. Both of his parents are still living. Roland feels that much of his childhood was spent attempting to reconcile the differences between his father and mother, whom he describes as being "real enemies to each other." On one occasion, in a marriage and family course, he volunteered to sculpt his family of origin. This means that he physically placed other students from the class in positions that reflected the family patterns of relationship in which he grew up. He placed a student in his mother's position, which was on one side of the classroom; and on the other side he placed a student in his father's position. This sculpted distance between his father and mother reflected what he perceived to be the emotional distance between his two parents, an emotional distance that caused Roland much pain in his life. This was obvious because of the expression on his face as he constructed the relationships in his family of origin.

Many factors contributed to the discord in Roland's family. One of the contributing influences was a thirty-year difference between his parent's ages. His mother was in her fifties and his father was in his eighties at the time of the counseling. Both parents worked hard all of their lives, and they looked to their children to provide them with some of their material needs, which included mortgage payments. In the context of parental expectations Roland felt that his role had always been to mediate the marital problems of his parents. He felt he was assigned the role of the marriage counselor to his parents, because they were always bringing their problems to him, and he felt like he was always in the middle of the problems. It was clear that Roland felt that his parents abdicated their own responsibility for themselves and their marriage, and that he was picked to fill the void. He felt his own needs for parenting were unmet and frustrated as a result. He felt trapped in the role, and although he was not living at home, and had not for a number of years, he felt that he carried his parents' conflict around inside him. He felt like he had no real self apart from that role and desired greatly to be free of his parents' conflict. He felt tired all the time and listless.

Roland did have very positive experiences in his childhood church home. There he felt accepted and found a place where he was challenged to grow. He recalled this experience with fond memories.

The Nature of the Self

It is clear from the case that Roland had a great deal of difficulty differentiating himself from his parental home. His sense of self, as a separate person in his own right, but significantly related to his parents, was severely impaired. His feeling of self-worth was very low because of this inability to differentiate himself.

The family dynamics were characterized by not-good-enough parenting reflected in the way he was used by his parents to solve their marital conflict. The parents were preoccupied with their own relationship and had little time to communicate to Roland in an attentive way that his need for their concern, free from the marital conflict, was primary. In the family system he had a difficult time feeling worthwhile as a unique person, and this affected his ability to develop as an autonomous person. The ability of the family to transmit the value of self-worth was impaired.

Roland was a religious person and found some surrogate parents in the caring church community. Although his lack of primary regard within his family of origin was the central dynamic in his sense of who he was, he found support and nurture within the caring community of the church, and learned that caring relationships were important. He also learned that the gospel challenged him to grow and develop as a person, and he sought to do this, but failed to do so because of his family-of-origin influence. It was at this point that he sought counseling. His goal was to nurture the seeds of self-worth planted by his early church experiences.

Creating a Context for the Exploration of Nurturing Images

It is not easy to create a context for the use of images in pastoral care. The use of images is the active exploration of the meaning of the dream image for the individual's growth. The most meaningful use of the dream image comes when the transference resistance or compliance is sufficiently resolved so that the person pursues the meaning of the image out of inner motivaton, and not to please or cooperate with me.

The transference in the case of Roland was initially in the form of compliance. He wanted to win my approval—because of his need to feel worthwhile—by appearing to be cooperative with the counseling process. However, this compliance was short-lived, and the resentment associated with playing the compliant game began to emerge. It was at this point that his full anger toward his parents' lack of adequate concern for him was brought into the relationship. This anger was brought on because I refused to gratify his need for approval, which is an important technique in depth pastoral counseling. The gratification of clients' wishes often prevents the client from discovering deep internal strengths and resources. Not gratifying his needs brought the real problem of his growth into the open, which was his anger over being stuck in his family of origin.

Roland dared not express his resentment and disappointment openly to the counselor. He expressed his negative feelings in passive ways by conveniently forgetting to keep his appointments. The counselor recognized this as transference resistance rather than compliance, and he confronted Roland with his avoidance pattern. The timing of the counselor's interpretation was right on target, and Roland not only expressed his resentment, but he also relished the opportunity to confront his inadequate "god." It was at this point in the counseling process that he began to realize that he had placed an unreal expectation upon the counselor. His willingness to express his real feelings helped him to experience the hurt and pain of growing up in his family of origin. He also began to accept that those days of frustration were gone and would have to be replaced by new relationships. It was at that point that a real collaborative relationship began, and he began to try to change his basic approach to life. He began to seek new relationships for satisfying his basic need for self-worth. This did not happen until the transference resistance was interpreted and worked through.

Freeing the Soul to Go in Search of Images

The working through of the transference enabled the soul of Roland to pursue images that could satisfy his strivings for self-worth. The collective unconscious became more available to him. He began to draw upon it in order to construct a new life based upon making a link between the collective unconscious and his conscious life. His soul became more active in his personality growth.

At this point in the counseling process he began to report dreams that reflected the emergence of the depth dimension of his personality. Analysis of his dreams began to show that a faceless woman was emerging as the central figure in the dreams. The meaning of this image was pursued by free association, which allowed him to probe the meaning of this image for his life. He would also identify with each object in the dream, living and non-living, as a way to get in touch with the meaning of the dream for him.

One dream out of a series of dreams deserves our special attention. He reported the following:

> I dreamed of a house that was hit by a tornado. Everybody was killed inside except an old man who was cleaning up after the damage had been done, and a faceless woman. I started to leave the scene of the accident of nature when the faceless

woman beckoned me back. I wanted to run. She said that my work wasn't done. She began to wave her hands in a beckoning manner, and I noticed that her hands were black. I went back to the scene and began to clean up.

He began to explore the meaning of the dream for himself. He said that the house represented his own condition at that time. He felt that it had been totally destroyed, but that the process of rebuilding had begun. It was pointed out to him that this dream had taken place at a time when he decided to give up his old family role assignment and his unrealistic expectations of the therapist. He picked up on this interpretation and explored more fully the meaning of the images in the dream. He identified the faceless woman with the black hands as his mother. He remembered something she had always tried to teach him. She had told him that no matter what he did, even if it were sweeping, was honest work. This was the first positive thing that he had ever said about his mother. The old man was the resource that was going to help him rebuild his life.

It is my feeling that this dream was a numinous dream. That is, the soul was free to find images that could lead him to his true salvation. It led him back to some nurturing images of mother that gave him the motivation to change his life and a new feeling of self-worth.

The numinous quality of the dream can be seen if we analyze in depth the meaning of mother image. For Carl Jung, the woman is the feminine side of the male personality. It also means the soul.[13] Its major characteristic is wisdom.[14] It is also a mother archetype or symbol that represents a numinous quality that points the longing of the soul for redemption, the kingdom of God and Heaven.[15] The dream had a similar meaning for Roland. For him the dream was one of maternal care and compassion. It was what supported and sustained his new pursuit of growth. It was also a second birth for him because it showed him a different side of his mother that gave him new life. However, this mother was more than his earthly mother. She was also his archetypal mother because she represented the vehicle through which God was working to bring new life to him. His real mother represented the manifest, or first level of, meaning of the dream, but the archetypal mother represented the deeper, numinous meaning of the dream. Indeed, this dream embodied numinous and religious resources that had transforming potential.

The dream enabled Roland to find the real source of his salvation. It chose an image out of the past that could satisfy his striving for true meaning. It also helped him to find satisfaction through nurture. The dream was also numinous in that it was the beginning of his new life, which was made possible by the soul's finding its true ground.

There were some concrete results of Roland's numinous experience. The first result was personal. It provided the necessary support that enabled him to surrender the security of old patterns so that he could take the risk of being an autonomous person. He held onto the old role of marriage counselor to parents because it provided a sense of comfort and warmth even though it was killing his personality. Yet, the image, along with the counseling relationship, provided enough security for him to make the separation from his family-of-origin pattern. The image and the counseling relationship took the place of the restricting role and provided the environment for the second birth.

The numinous experience also enabled him to be a real participant in his family as an adult. Some think that one must reject one's family in order to develop one's sense of self as a separate person. This rejection is characteristic of people who do not have a secure sense of self, and this rigid stance is an attempt to protect the fragile, undeveloped self. However, people with a secure sense of self do not seek to isolate themselves from others, but they seek to engage others on a deeper level. This was the case with Roland. He began to make trips home to spend time with his parents in order to tell them how much he loved them and to do things for them *he wanted* to do. He gave up his lifelong goal to raise them, and he began to accept them as they were. This gave him a great deal of freedom, and he was able to enjoy an in-depth relationship with them he had not previously experienced. He was able to relate to them out of love rather than out of a mandate imposed by a childhood role. He no longer viewed his parents as victimizers.

The numinous experience not only helped him change his attitude toward and relationship with his parents, it also helped him change his attitude and relationship to God. He had confined his view of life to his counseling role to his parents. As a result, he experienced God as distant, authoritarian, unapproachable, and impersonal. However, when the dream helped him focus on the true source of his soul's striving, his attitude toward God changed. Rather than perceiving and experiencing God as authoritarian who cared little for him as a person, he began to experience God as one who sought him and who communicated with him. He began to feel and know that God did not ignore him, but that he was personal. He also began to realize that God worked through his personal dispositions and abilities rather than opposed them. He found that he was not rejected, but was accepted as one of God's own creations. God was no longer a military commander issuing orders, but became an approachable guide who led him to new heights of growth and development.

IMPLICATIONS OF THE CASE FOR VALUE FORMATION

The case study has specific implications for the transmission of values. In the most general sense the counseling relationship had the impact of rekindling values that were part of Roland's early childhood socialization experience within the accepting environment of the church. Beyond this socialization or the internalization of values as a result of participation in a caring community, the counseling relationship nurtured a context for experiencing the transcendent in Roland's life that facilitated new meaning that reinforced old values. Counseling contributed to a conjunctive process of value formation. The old values lying dormant within Roland's socialized history were rejuvenated, and the experience of the numinous dream reinforced and enlivened the values and gave new meaning to them.

Through the counseling relationship, Roland's sense of worth as a person who could grow into a unique individual related significantly to himself, others, and God, was experienced in a way that confirmed the transcendent quality of values. Prior to his encounter with the numinous dream image or mother archetype, he thought of the values as transitory and easily lost. He thought they had lost their significance and power to bestow meaning. However, experiencing old values on a transcendent level stamped indelibly on Roland's mind the durable nature of the foundation of his feelings of worthwhileness as a person, the vitality of forces inherent in life supporting his capacity to grow into a separate and unique person, the necessity of caring relationships for the fulfillment of personhood, and the role of God working through others and the unconscious to communicate love and concern to him. These values were experienced existentially at the core of his being and not at the abstract level.

Modernity, with its emphasis upon removing a sense of the transcendent from cultural symbols, contributed to the experience of the transitory quality of values in Roland's life. However, numinous dream images, when explored, bestowed a different and enduring dimension of values for Roland. Indeed, when the transcendent is not supported by a cultural world-view, it does not mean that it does not exist. Rather, the transcendent and the values associated with it begin to manifest themselves more forcibly through the collective unconscious.

CHAPTER 9

Image Exploration and Marriage Counseling

In the last chapter we explored how numinous images help bring a sense of continuity to values that were experienced in community early in one's life. This chapter will examine the role of the numinous image in strengthening the nomos-building functions of marriage. The nomos-building function of marriage is creating an atmosphere that allows marital partners to see themselves as people of inestimable worth, capable of growth and development related significantly to each other, to others, and to God.

According to Peter Berger, nomos-building deals with a consistent reality or a social world that can be meaningfully experienced by individuals.[1] This reality is rooted in community and is transmitted in and through concrete relationships, through constant dialogue and caring interaction. The values associated with the consistent reality are ordered and given constancy by the community and are reinforced through community ritual life and symbols. As people participate in the community, they encounter and partake of the life of the values, and these values help to give meaning to life.

The exploration of images from the unconscious life of the marital partners can enliven and reinforce this value-formation process. According to Berger, the process of constructing a social world begins with subjectively experienced meanings becoming externalized in interactions with others.[2] In marriage, the partners are called upon not only to mediate wider community values, but also to enhance and enliven these values with the values that emerge from subjective experiences. How numinous images emanating from the collective unconscious converge with the community values will be explored.

Numinous images are vehicles of universal meaning and often emerge to give strength to past values. Numinous images are also the values that are part of one's own racial and historical past and that give meaning to life. They are an embodiment of the transcendent and convey the external dimension supporting the values. Given these historical, universal, and transcendent qualities experienced on the subjective level, image exploration gives a foundation to community values. They have a dimension beyond the community, and enrich marriages when they are explored. There is a dimension to value formation beyond the social construction of reality.[3]

The nomos-building function is not only related to mediating values rooted in the larger community; it also involves creating a context for new meaning to emerge when past relationships do not convey the values adequately. In this context, the nomos-building function becomes more significant. For example, Berger points out that marriage and the family were once woven into a wider community network where the flow of values was stable and taken for granted. Now, according to Berger:

> Unlike an earlier situation in which the establishment of the marriage simply added to the differentiation and complexity of an already existing social world, marriage partners in today's society are embarked on the often difficult task of construction for themselves the little world in which they will live. To be sure, the larger society provides them with certain standard instructions as to how they should go about this task, but this does not change the fact that considerable effort of their own is required for its realization.[4]

The nomos-building process is a process of continual definition and redefinition. This is why communication skills and self-differentiation are so important. Lack of adequate communication and self-differentiation blocks the definition and redefinition process that is so crucial in developing a joint world-view that gives meaning to the couple's relationship.

Each couple brings a world-view and values from his or her own family, and these ingredients are transformed into a new, dialectical, redefining process known as *codefining* in the marital relationship. Each person's past world-view is reworked and reinterpreted into an integrated view of reality.[5] Lack of self-differentiation by the marriage partners blocks this process.

CASE STUDY

David and Mary Strong have been married for thirty years. David was 56 and Mary was 53 at the time they came for counseling. The presenting problem was that she suspected that her husband was having an affair, because she felt he was no longer interested in her. He said that this wasn't true; he affirmed his love for her, and said her problems were due to the middle-age change. He seemed unwilling to be intimate in terms of sharing feelings, and she would blame and attack him constantly and accuse him of not loving her, and a vicious cycle developed. The more she blamed and attacked, the more he withdrew; and the more he withdrew, the more she blamed and attacked.

Their family history revealed an interesting family situation. Mary's father and mother were divorced. She was one of ten children, and was the fifth child. Her mother had a hard time raising them alone, and relied on Mary to raise the children who were younger than she. Her mother was often sick, and Mary had to drop out of school in order to take care of the mother and younger children. She married at fifteen in order to get out from under this situation.

David grew up as a part of a sharecropper's family. He felt

like he was the black sheep of the family and never mattered to his mother or sisters. He worked for his father in the fields and never received any money from him and felt used as a result. He was hired out to white families but never saw the money. He felt like he had had to raise himself and he resented this.

In her family of origin, Mary was assigned the role of child-mother and David played the role of an angry, neglected child. In many ways they were victims of the family roles that were placed upon them as children. David seemed to be forced into a role that would enable the father to maintain his self-image as the head of the house, which frustrated a sense of autonomy in David. Mary's role appears to have been assigned because of pure family necessity. However, her being chosen when there were other older siblings at home points to the possibility that she was carrying out an unconscious expectation of her mother.

Both Mary and David's childhood experiences forced them to behave in ways consistent with their families' expectations. Moreover, their respective roles were reinforced by family myths and rules that made it impossible to escape the expectations. As a result, the roles became the center around which they organized their personalities, their attitudes, and their behavior.

Because the role became the center of their lives and the concomittant attitudes and behavior persisted into adulthood, they could not give them up. Although they were adults, they were not able to escape the trap of the family. They were not individuated or differentiated from their families. They were still "children," not able to know themselves apart from the families in which they were born. Maturity begins when one is able to differentiate oneself from the family and to know who one is apart from the family. Not being able to individuate in this way blocks growth and contributes to one's low self-esteem.

When childhood role assignments persist into adulthood without alteration, they influence the selection of a mate. Somehow the role assignments propel people unconsciously to select mates who either reinforce or repudiate the roles played in the family of origin. David and Mary duplicated their family roles. Their respective family histories led them to pick a mate who would enable them to recapture the security of a world that was lost. Thus, Mary needed a child to raise as she attempted to recreate her family-of-origin role, and David needed a parent who would neglect him as his father did in his family of origin. Indeed, Mary had a son in her husband, and David had a parent in Mary who nagged and neglected him.

Although Mary and David strove to recreate their family of origin, this did not satisfy their spiritual needs. All of their energy went into making sure that the families they left behind were recreated, because they were unable to individuate and differentiate themselves from their families. Therefore, they did not use their energies to find a source of growth and strength that transcended their families of origin. They confined their need for meaning and growth to old patterns and did not search for new potential for growth and meaning apart from the family-of-origin patterns. They sought to remain children, resting secure in knowing that they were in familiar territory. They preferred the security of Egyptian bondage rather than insecure freedom to grow and expand.

However, after thirty years of marriage, they realized that they had to make a change in their married lives. This came about because their youngest child left home as an adult and previously unmet needs resurfaced and manifested themselves anew. They had not disappeared in thirty years. They just remained dormant while Mary invested herself in her children and David worked hard to make ends meet. However, the last child's growing up and leaving and David's early retirement forced them to depend upon each other, and there were no side distractions. They had to confront the barrenness of their relationship. Realizing the desperateness of the situation, they sought marriage counseling.

From a nomos-building perspective, the lack of differentiation from their families of origin prevented the building of a meaningful relationship based on respect for the worth and growth of the other. Each used the other to fulfill the family-of-origin expectations, and they did not fulfill the nomic function of their life together. There was no real reworking of their past biographies into a new integrated pattern that gave meaning to their married life. Each person's identity was frozen into a pattern of relating that dwarfed self-expression. In a word, their relationship was frustrating. Both needed to be liberated so that they could be free to participate wholly in the relationship and make a contribution to the nomos-building function.

Marriage Counseling Methods

When David and Mary went for marriage counseling, the problem was assessed in much the same way as in the previous section. The recommendation was that they be counseled together, although the focus would be on individuation and differentiation from their family-of-origin expectations. This meant that the focus would not be on their marital relationship, except when marital expectations resembled the family-of-origin expectations. Thus, the method of therapy used with the Strongs was in-depth couple therapy with each spouse while the other spouse was present.

Murray Bowen's method of couple therapy was utilized, in which the therapist directs the interchange.[6] The counselor directed to himself the communication that would have normally been directed to the other spouse. The spouses were not allowed to talk to each other in the session. They had to talk to the counselor. In this way, intense emotional conflict was lessened between the couple, and this enabled one spouse to hear what the other spouse was really saying and feeling. It also gave the listening spouse a chance to see how the counselor became a role model for the listening spouse. In this form of counseling, the other spouse was not left out; he or she was drawn in by the counselor at crucial points. The counselor either chose to give both equal time or allowed one person to be the focus of the session.

Using this direct communication method, the counselor could effectively do individual counseling as well as marriage counseling with the couple. It also facilitated drawing in important insights that had relevance to the marital relationship.

Another important advantage of this method involves the transference phenomenon. In general, each spouse will try to create the same dynamics in the counseling relationship that exist in the marriage. If the marital problems are a reflection of the family-of-origin difficulties, then the counseling relationship also becomes the stage on which family problems are recreated. In other words, there may be a dual transference. Each spouse could attempt to recreate within the counseling relationship the dynamics that existed in the family of origin and in the marriage. The skill of the counselor in interpreting these dynamics at the right time is a key to resolving this marital dual transference.

The Bowen method also enables the therapist to use images in the therapy process. The dream image is often a tremendous resource for assessing the current level of personality functioning, as well as the inherent resources for helping the person achieve emancipation from bondage to the family of origin. Therefore, the self, which is locked into the family role, may find resources within to sustain it while the person seeks to individuate from his or her family.

The dream also enables bringing spiritual resources to bear upon the current crisis. The images or forms that appear in the dream are often sources for solutions as well as sustenance while the person works on solutions. Therefore the therapist cannot ignore the dream, because it can enable the soul to bring resources into the personality for growth.

Helpful methods of dream image interpretation are (1) attempting to understand the circumstances and the waking events immediately surrounding the dream, (2) exploring the various meanings the dreamer sees in the dream, (3) exploring each image in the dream, both animate and inanimate, for its potential meaning, and (4) helping the counselor identify with the images, objects, and personages to plumb the depth of their meaning. Following is a case study in which some of these methods were used to help the Strongs free their selves for self-actualization, and free their souls to bring spiritual resources to their selves.

CASE STUDY OF IMAGE EXPLORATION IN MARRIAGE COUNSELING

In counseling, David and Mary's dreams were used throughout to help them find resources and solutions from the unconscious for their problems. It was very difficult to establish a collaborative relationship with David in the beginning of the counseling relationship, because he defended against intimacy or being related to the process on a feeling level. On the other hand, Mary was very cooperative, and her willing cooperation soon drew David into the counseling process.

After the fifteenth session, Mary began to complain that she felt her husband had been holding her back from the things she needed and wanted to do for herself. Up until this time the counseling had concentrated on the difficulty Mary was having letting her 17-year-old son go, while David talked about his fears associated with early retirement. During this fifteenth session, Mary reported the following dream. (The issue was letting go, because letting go would mean changes in the way they related.)

She dreamed that she was in the entrance of a tunnel, and at the end of the tunnel there were two white-robed, hooded men carrying a box that had a light encircling it. She said that as she gazed at the box, her husband suddenly appeared before her with a look of fear on his face.

Following the basic principles of dream interpretation, the counselor solicited from Mary what she felt the dream meant. She said the dream was extremely frightening to her because her mother had said that a small box with a light surrounding it meant death. Somehow, she felt that this dream was a forecast of her imminent physical death. The counselor accepted Mary's anxiety about death and asked her to explore further what she meant by death. She didn't feel like pursuing the theme of death in the dream—she changed the focus and began to talk about the marriage, saying that it had taken the best years of her life. She was not conscious of her change of subject, but it was obvious that her unconscious made a connection between the theme of death and the marriage. Thus, the change in focus revealed the logic of the unconscious, which linked the fear of death to a frustrating marriage.

When Mary moved away from the dream and began to talk about the marriage, the counselor sought to involve David in the counseling process. He asked David if he had any responses to the dream. He replied positively, and began to talk about how she blamed him for her predicament in life. He pointed out that he had tried to block her early in their marriage; however, since he had recognized how unhappy she was, he had tried to push her to fulfill some of her career goals. He said that she had confused him in that the harder he pushed her to do something that might fulfill her, the more she resented him. He indicated that he had become tired of being confused and had come to the conclusion that she was scared to move forward into doing what she wanted.

The counselor turned to Mary again and began to explore with her the reluctance that her husband identified. She was very resentful and angry at what David had said. However, after her initial anger, she began to explore her real fear of pursuing what she had always wanted to do.

In the next two weeks Mary enrolled in night school and began to prepare for her high school equivalency examination. After registering for school, she reported the following dream. She said she saw a square about the size of a large door. The square was made up of little squares. In the middle of the large square was a small square in which she saw the face of Abraham Lincoln. In the top square, she saw the word "all." She emphasized that "all" had three letters, and that they were capitalized. The counselor asked her what the dream meant to her. She said, "Well, I guess I have missed the boat again." The counselor was puzzled and asked for clarification. She went back to the dream of the tunnel, and said that she thought she missed out on the treasure that was held by the two men in white robes. In this response, her attitude toward the box had changed; it was no longer a symbol of death, but a symbol of rebirth. The counselor noted in his mind her change of emphasis regarding the box, and he then moved to another image in the dream. He asked her about the image of Lincoln that was in the square. He felt that Lincoln's image might unlock the meaning of both dreams. She pointed out that Lincoln freed the slaves. When she said this, a light came upon her face, and she said, "I see the meaning of the dream. I am liberated from my bondage." She then went on to explore how good she felt being in school, and how much better she felt about herself. The dream, therefore, was a sign to her conscious mind that something significant had taken place in her life. She was liberated or on the way to liberation, and her husband agreed with her interpretation. She no longer felt blocked.

Mary's growth influenced David's growth. When she began to pursue her own deeply felt goals, he too began to find joy in giving her support, while at the same time exploring in counseling his relationship with his family of origin. He too was able to find significant images in his dreams that pointed to his resolving issues related to his family of origin. His dreams often took him back to his early childhood in the home, and an image of a significant male appeared in many of his dreams as a guide through some of the crucial growing pains of adolescents. This male image that appeared in his dreams helped him disentangle himself from the pain of his family origin, and at the same time helped him accept the limitations of his parents. As a result of this image, he began to feel worthwhile as a person and to change the image of himself as a neglected child. Thus, as a result of encountering this image he was able to become an adult partner relating to his self-actualizing wife in new ways.

THE SIGNIFICANCE OF IMAGES IN THE MARRIAGE CASE STUDY

The two dreams of Mary are extremely fruitful for analysis. The first dream of the tunnel is of great importance when analyzed from archetypal theory. Archetypal theory looks for universal images that have appeared with great frequency in the history of humanity. In this light, the dream, the tunnel could be interpreted as an entrance to the womb or the symbol of the second birth. This interpretation has further credence when the symbol of wholeness appeared represented in the box as well as in the circle of light. The number four, the circle, and light all reflect wholeness. Thus, in Mary's dream, these archetypal symbols pointed to potential new birth. However, the potential was not actualized. Mary had to actualize it by deciding to remove the obstacle that stood in the way of her rebirth. Her reluctance to take a step to embrace a new life was the obstacle. When she made a choice to move, her liberation came. That is, her liberation dream occurred when she had decided to take a step toward self-actualization by registering in school. The dreamer, then, holds the key. The counselor (skilled) facilitates the process. Both work together. One cannot do it without the aid of the other.

Mary was right in her interpretation that the box was a symbol of death. However, it was a sign of liberating death rather than physical death. It meant that the old image of herself as a glorified, unrewarded servant of others had to die before a new self-image could be born. In Jungian archetypal theory, the second birth is often preceded by death. Psychologically and spiritually something must die before something else can live.

The death and rebirth theme is also a central theme of major world religions. As such, this theme has universal significance, and Mary was drawing upon a universal reservoir of resources.

In the second dream, the square, or the number four as represented by four sides, appeared again as in the case of the box in the first dream. However, this time the number three appeared, represented by three letters in the word "all." In archetypal theory, three is also a symbol of wholeness. Thus, wholeness was again the theme of the dream.

The second dream was different from the first dream, however. The first dream pointed to the possibility of wholeness or of the second birth. However, the second dream was an announcement that wholeness had been achieved, that the second birth was a reality, and that liberation from bondage had occurred. Thus, the unconscious announced the Good News that liberation of the self and soul had occurred. The second dream was a declaration that there was an inner transformation. It proclaimed that Mary was now internally free from her family-of-origin problems and from the attitude that prevented her from achieving self-actualization. The second dream acted as a messenger bringing news that something significant had taken place.

As this case study has shown, dreams are extremely significant for marriage counseling. They have diagnostic value as well as therapeutic and curative value. They can be used just as effectively in couple therapy as in individual therapy. Each spouse can benefit from being present. When dreams are interpreted and analyzed in counseling, they can enrich the lives of both partners as well as giving the one partner a view of the other's secret self. Beyond this, the spouse can add meaning to the dream that the other partner might have ignored.

The crucial finding of the image exploration was that it began the process of nomos-building when they began to redefine their past biographies. They were now free to begin to reconstruct a new view of reality based on a new appreciation of each other's uniqueness and worth. They also were free to enjoy their interaction and relationship. They began to grow and build significant relationships with their families that added to their sense of identity as unique persons as well as as a couple. They also began to integrate the subjective dream images into their communication and this brought added meaning to their relationship. Thus, counseling helped to lay the groundwork for the experience of meaning at a profound level where the dream image played a significant part in nomos-building.

Throughout this book the emphasis has been placed upon the holistic nature of pastoral care and counseling. They are part of a larger ministry of the total church. As an extension of the ministry of the church, the holistic nature of individuals must be part of the theory of pastoral care and counseling. Moreover, the value, moral, and spiritual dimensions of people's lives and of the caring community must not be ignored. Indeed, they are essential aspects of pastoral care and counseling. As a ministry of the church, pastoral care and counseling receive their resources from the caring community as well as from the rich spiritual resources that work through the inner lives of people. The behavioral sciences can help the church with its value and spiritual task as long as they serve the ends of the mission of the church.

Modernity is a vital force in society and in the black church. It is hoped that this book has provided one approach to holding onto and recapturing the soul and value dimensions of our lives together in families and within the church.

NOTES

PREFACE

1. Peter Berger called this technological process and the dislodging of values and beliefs modernization. See *Facing Up to Modernity* (New York: Basic Books, 1977), p. 70.

2. This is Thomas Luckmann's thesis in *The Invisible Religion* (New York: The Macmillan Co., 1967).

3. The black power movement and the black awareness movement were partially a response to the integration movement. Separatism was very much part of the movements, and this in part was a rejection of melting pot conformism. One did not have to become white to be somebody. See James Cone, *Black Theology and Black Power* (New York: The Seabury Press, 1969), pp. 17-20. Major J. Jones, *Black Awareness: A Theology of Hope* (Nashville: Abingdon Press, 1971), pp. 69-71. Albert B. Cleage, Jr., *Black Christian Nationalism* (New York: William Morrow & Co., 1972), p. xii.

4. Berger, *Facing Up to Modernity*, pp. 132-34.

5. *Ibid.*, pp. 5-7.

CHAPTER 1: COUNSELING AND PERSONALITY

1. Olin P. Moyd, *Redemption in Black Theology* (Valley Forge, Pa.: Judson Press, 1979), p. 28.

2. For further development of this point see Edward P. Wimberly, "A Conceptual Model for Pastoral Care in the Black Church Utilizing Systems and Crisis Theories" (Ph.D. dissertation, Ann Arbor, Michigan, University Microfilms, 1976), pp. 5-6.

3. See *Narrative of Sojourner Truth* (Boston: J. B. Yerrington and Son, 1850); see also George Rawick, *The American Slave: A Composite Autobiography* (Westport, Connecticut: Greenwood Publishing Co., 1972), vol. 3, parts 3-4, pp. 5-7 and 152-56.

4. See the following book for definitions and development of these four dimensions: Robert R. Carkhuff and Bernard G. Berenson, *Beyond*

Counseling and Therapy (New York: Holt, Rinehart & Winston, 1967), pp. 23-43.

5. William W. Everett and T. J. Bachmeyer, *Disciplines in Transformation: A Guide to Theology and the Behavioral Sciences* (Washington, D.C.: University Press of America, 1979), pp. 3-13.

6. Ludwig von Bertalanffy, "General Systems Theory and Psychiatry: An Overview," in *General Systems Theory and Psychiatry,* eds. W. Gray, F. Duhl, and N. Rizzo (Boston: Little, Brown, 1969), p. 37.

7. Portions of this section originally appeared in the *Journal of The Interdenominational Theological Center* 3 (Spring 76), pp. 28-35.

8. Ruth Caplan, *Psychiatry and the Community in the 19th Century* (New York: Basic Books, 1969).

9. See Melville J. Herskovits, *The Myth of the Negro Past* (Gloucester, Mass.: Peter Smith, 1970).

10. John Mbiti, *African Religions and Philosophy* (Garden City, New York: Doubleday & Co., 1970), p. 20.

11. Cedrick Clark, "Black Studies or the Study of Black People," in *Black Psychology,* ed. Reginald Jones (New York: Harper & Row, 1972), p. 11.

12. Mbiti, *African Religions and Philosophy,* p. 154.

13. Thomas J. Pugh and Emily Mudd, "Attitudes of Black Women and Men Toward Using Community Service," *Journal of Religion and Health* 10 (July 1971), pp. 256-77.

14. Stephen Ring, "Attitude Toward Mental Illness and Use of Care-Takers in the Black Community," *American Journal of Orthopsychiatry* 40 (July 1970), p. 711.

15. Barbara Lerner, *Therapy in the Ghetto* (Baltimore: Johns Hopkins University Press, 1972), p. 10.

16. For the significance of images in the black experience see Clifton H. Johnson, ed., *God Struck Me Dead: Religious Conversion Experiences of Ex-Slaves* (Philadelphia: Pilgrim Press, 1969); and Anne E. Wimberly, "Spirituals as Symbolic Expression," *Journal of the Interdenominational Theological Center* 5 (Fall 1977), pp. 23-32.

17. See the example cited by Albert Raboteau, *Slave Religion: The Invisible Institution in the Antebellum South* (New York: Oxford University Press, 1978), p. 255.

18. This definition of personality reflects the following contributions. Ludwig von Bertalanffy, *General Systems Theory* (New York: George Braziller, 1968); "General Systems Theory and Psychiatry," in *American Handbook of Psychiatry,* vol. III, S. Arieti, ed. (New York: Basic Books, 1966), pp. 705-21.

19. This view of the self reflects the work of Heinz Kohut in *The Restoration of the Self* (New York: International Universities Press, 1977). In this work the self is viewed as more than the psychic apparatus of id, ego, and superego. It is the center of the whole personality.

The social interactive dimension of the self is reflected in the work by Gerard Chrzanowski, *Interpersonal Approach to Psychoanalysis: Contemporary View of Harry Stack Sullivan* (New York: Gardner Press, 1977).

The spiritual view of the self is largely a contribution of my study of the slave narrative experiences, particularly the conversion tradition. Also the insights from Jung, especially in his autobiography, *Memories, Dreams,*

Reflections (New York: Vintage Books, 1965), have contributed to my understanding of the spiritual nature of the self.

20. Erik Erikson, *Childhood and Society* (New York: W. W. Norton & Co., 1963), pp. 268-69.

21. This is George H. Mead's understanding of the self. For further details see Herbert Blummer, *Symbolic Interactionism: Perspective and Method* (Englewood Cliffs, New Jersey: Prentice-Hall, 1969), pp. 62-64.

22. This notion of the soul is built upon Thomas Merton's concept of final integration. See "Final Integration," in *Conversion: Perspectives on Personal and Social Transformation,* ed. Walter E. Conn (New York: Alba House, 1978), pp. 263-72. See also James Hillman, *In Search: Psychology and Religion* (New York: Charles Scribner's Sons, 1967), pp. 40-43.

CHAPTER 2: THE RECOVERY OF THE SOUL

1. Charles Gerkin, *Crisis Experience in Modern Life: Theory and Theology for Pastoral Care* (Nashville: Abingdon, 1979), p. 16.

2. Edward P. Wimberly, "A Conceptual Model for Pastoral Care in the Black Church Utilizing Systems and Crisis Theories" (Ann Arbor: University Microfilms, 1976), pp. 35-36.

3. See Clifton H. Johnson, ed., *God Struck Me Dead;* and George Rawick, ed., *The American Slave: A Composite Autobiography,* vols. 1–19 (Westport, Connecticut: Greenwood Publishing Co., 1972).

4. Newbell Niles Puckett, *Folk Beliefs of the Southern Negro* (Chapel Hill: University of North Carolina Press, 1926), p. 110.

5. Carl Jung, *Modern Man's Search for a Soul* (New York: Harcourt Brace Jovanovich, 1933), p. 229.

6. Erik H. Erikson, *Childhood and Society,* 2nd. (New York: W. W. Norton & Co., 1963), pp. 268-69.

7. Erich Fromm, *Psychoanalysis and Religion* (New Haven: Yale University Press, 1972), p. 6.

8. William Hulme, *Pastoral Care Come of Age* (Nashville: Abingdon Press, 1970).

9. Gerald G. May, "The Psychodynamics of Spirituality: A Follow-Up," in *The Journal of Pastoral Care,* 31 (June, 1977), pp. 84-85.

10. See Linda Bourque, "Social Correlations of Transcendental Experiences" (Ann Arbor: University Microfilms International, 1968). See also Alister Hardy, *The Spiritual Nature of Man* (Oxford: Clarendon Press, 1979).

11. Archie Smith, Jr., "The Meaning of Spirituality: In the Preparation for Life: An Empirical Approach," *Encounter* (Spring, 1979).

12. Ernest Becker, *The Denial of Death* (New York: The Free Press, 1973), pp. 176-207.

13. Ira Progoff, *Jung's Psychology and Its Social Meaning* (Garden City, New York: Anchor Books, 1973), p. 199. See also Jung, *Modern Man in Search of Soul,* p. 215.

14. Herbert Blumer, *Symbolic Interactionism: Perspective and Method* (Englewood Cliffs, New Jersey: Prentice-Hall, 1969), p. 12.

15. Peter Berger, *Facing Up to Modernity* (New York: Basic Books, 1977), pp. 70-80.

16. May, "The Psychodynamics of Spirituality," p. 87.

17. See Thomas Luckmann, *The Invisible Religion* (New York: The Macmillan Co., 1970), p. 98.

18. Becker, *The Denial of Death*, p. 280.

19. Erich Fromm, *Psychoanalysis and Religion* (New Haven: Yale University Press, 1972), p. 72.

20. *Ibid.*, p. 3.

21. Progoff, *Jung's Psychology*, p. 15.

22. Luckmann, *The Invisible Religion*, p. 70.

23. William A. Clebsch and Charles R. Jaekle, *Pastoral Care in Historical Perspective* (New York: Jason Aronson, 1975).

24. May, "The Psychodynamics of Spirituality," p. 88.

CHAPTER 3: HOLISM IN THE FAMILY

1. This argument is developed in the following article. Lois N. Glasser and Paul H. Glasser, "Hedonism and the Family: Conflict in Values?" in *Journal of Marriage and Family Counseling*, vol. 3 (October, 1977), pp. 11-18.

2. Harold H. Titus, *Living Issues in Philosophy* (New York: Van Nostrand Reinhold Co., 1970), p. 481.

3. *Ibid.*, p. 230.

4. For a summary of the view of these three men see Salvatore R. Maddi, *Personality Theories: A Comparative Analysis* (Homewood, Ill.: The Dorsey Press, 1976), pp. 48-58.

5. Glasser, "Hedonism," pp. 12-14.

6. Charles Frankel, "The Impact of Changing Values on the Family," *Social Casework*, vol. 57 (June, 1976), p. 360.

7. Gibson Winter, *Love and Conflict: New Patterns in Family Life* (Garden City, New York: Dolphin Books, 1961), p. 21.

8. Philip Slater, *Earthwalk* (Garden City, New York: Doubleday & Co., 1974), p. 27.

9. Herbert G. Gutman, *The Black Family in Slavery and Freedom 1750-1925* (New York: Vintage Books, 1976), pp. 466-67.

10. Elmer P. Martin and Joanne Mitchell Martin, *The Black Extended Family* (Chicago: The University of Chicago Press, 1978), p. 2.

11. Charles Stewart, *The Minister As Family Counselor* (Nashville: Abingdon, 1979), pp. 37-38.

12. Ira Progoff, *Jung's Psychology and Its Social Meaning* (Garden City, New York: Doubleday & Co., 1973), p. 15.

13. Carl Jung, *Archetypes of the Collective Unconscious* (Princeton, New Jersey: Princeton University Press), p. 66.

14. Progoff, *Jung's Psychology*, p. 242.

15. John A Sanford, *Dreams: God's Forgotten Language* (Philadelphia: J. B. Lippincott Co., 1968), p. 133.

16. Jung, *Archetypes*, p. 161.

17. *Ibid.*, p. 164.

18. Hans Schaer, *Religion and the Cure of a Soul in Jung's Psychology* (New York: Pantheon Books, 1950), p. 19.

19. *Ibid.*, pp. 80-89. The whole process of symbol formation is described in this section.

20. Carl G. Jung, *The Symbolic Life* (Princeton, New Jersey: Princeton University Press, 1976), p. 259.

21. Morton Kelsey, *The Other Side of Silence: A Guide to Christian Meditation* (New York: Paulist Press, 1976), pp. 125-208.

22. Clifton A. Johnson, ed., *God Struck Me Dead: Religious Conversion Experiences of Ex-Slaves* (Philadelphia: Pilgrim Press, 1969).

CHAPTER 4: SOCIOLOGY

1. Peter Berger, *Facing Up to Modernity* (New York: Basic Books, 1977), p. 134.

2. Edward P. Wimberly, *Pastoral Care in the Black Church* (Nashville: Abingdon, 1979), p. 34.

3. Milton Yinger, *Religion, Society, and the Individual: An Introduction to the Sociology of Religion* (New York: The Macmillan Co., 1969), pp. 75-76.

4. Luckmann, *The Invisible Religion*, pp. 69-70.

5. *Ibid.*, p. 73.

6. Berger, *Facing Up to Modernity*, p. 78.

7. *Ibid.*, p. 70.

8. Peter Berger and Thomas Luckmann, *The Social Construction of Reality* (Garden City, New York: Doubleday & Co., 1967), p. 130.

9. William A. Clebsch and Charles R. Jaekle, *Pastoral Care in Historical Perspective* (New York: Jason Aronson, 1975), p. 19.

10. Luckmann, *Invisible Religion*, p. 98.

11. For an in-depth discussion of this point, see Thomas C. Oden, "Recovering Lost Identity," in *The Journal of Pastoral Care*, vol. 34 (March 1980), pp. 4-19.

12. Berger, *Facing Up to Modernity*, p. 160.

13. *Ibid.*, p. 190.

14. *Ibid.*, p. 202.

15. Edward P. Wimberly, "A Conceptual Model for Pastoral Care in the Black Church Utilizing Systems and Crises Theories" (Ph.D. dissertation, Ann Arbor, Michigan, 1976), p. 42.

16. The following works are a small illustration of the five trends in pastoral care and counseling. Don S. Browning, *The Moral Context of Pastoral Care* (Philadelphia: Westminster Press, 1976); W. Clebsch and C. Jaekle, *Pastoral Care in Historical Perspective* (New York: Jason Aronson, 1975); Morton Kelsey, *The Other Side of Silence* (New York: Paulist Press, 1976): *Dreams: A Way to Listen to God* (New York: Paulist Press, 1978); Mansell Pattison, *Pastor and Parish—A Systems Approach* (Philadelphia: Fortress Press, 1977); Charles Gerkin, *Crisis Experience in Modern Life* (Nashville: Abingdon, 1979); Charles Stewart; *The Minister As Marriage Counselor* (Nashville: Abingdon, 1979); William Hulme, *Pastoral Care Come of Age* (Nashville: Abingdon Press, 1970); John Cobb, *Theology of Pastoral Care* (Philadelphia: Fortress Press, 1977); William H. Willimon, *Worship as Pastoral Care* (Nashville: Abingdon, 1979).

CHAPTER 5: SUPPORT SYSTEMS

1. Morris Taggart, "The Professionalization of the Parish Pastoral Counselor," *Journal of Pastoral Care*, vol. 27 (September 1973), p. 186.

2. A perspective on these three issues can be found in Hulme, *Pastoral Care Come of Age.*

3. This definition of community mental health is found in Gerald Caplan, *Principles of Preventive Psychiatry* (New York: Basic Books, 1964), p. 26.

4. For an extensive examination of the relationship of community mental health and the church, see Ruth Caplan, *Helping Helpers to Help* (New York: Seabury Press, 1972); Howard J. Clinebell, Jr., ed., *Community Mental Health: The Role of Church and Temple* (Nashville: Abingdon Press, 1970); Glenn Whitlock, *Preventive Psychology and the Church* (Philadelphia: Westminster Press, 1973).

5. Gerald Caplan examines the role of support systems in *Support Systems and Community Mental Health* (New York: Behavioral Publications, 1974).

6. *Ibid.*, p. 5.

7. *Ibid.*, pp. 25-26.

8. *Ibid.*, p. 4.

9. Elisabeth Kübler-Ross, *On Death and Dying* (New York: Collier-Macmillan Ltd., 1969), p. 99.

10. *Ibid.*, p. 34.

11. Erich Lindemann, "Symptomatology and Management of Acute Grief," *The American Journal of Psychiatry,* vol. 101 (September, 1944), p. 143.

CHAPTER 6: FAMILY DYNAMICS

1. See ch. 3, pp. 62-63.

2. Robert Staples, "Towards a Sociology of the Black Family: A Theoretical Assessment," in *Journal of Marriage and the Family,* vol. 33 (February, 1971), p. 133.

3. See National Urban League Project, *A Selected Annotated Bibliography on Black Families* (New York: 1977), p. 23; and particularly Margaret Lawrence, *Young Inner City Families: Development of Ego Strength Under Stress* (New York: Behavioral Publications, 1975).

4. For more details about the relevance of the systems perspective to counseling black families, see Denis A. Bagarozzi, "Family Therapy and the Black Middle Class: A Neglected Area of Study," in *Journal of Marital and Family Therapy,* vol. 6 (April, 1980), p. 160.

5. Vincent D. Foley, "Family Therapy with Black Disadvantaged Families," in *Journal of Marriage and Family* (January, 1975), pp. 29-38.

6. Salvador Minuchin, *et al., Families of the Slums* (New York: Basic Books, 1967).

7. See Edward P. Wimberly, *Pastoral Care in the Black Church* (Nashville: Abingdon, 1979), pp. 65-70. Here it must be added that lines of demarcation do not refer to physical distance or complete separation. Rather they refer to integrity functioning.

8. Bagarozzi in "Family Therapy and the Black Middle Class" (p. 16) disagrees with this statement. He says black family roles in middle class black families are egalitarian.

9. Salvador Minuchin, *Families and Family Therapy* (Cambridge: Harvard University Press, 1974), p. 51.

10. Virginia Satir, *Conjoint Family Therapy* (Palo Alto, Calif.: Science and Behavior Books, 1967), pp. 8-14; and *People-making* (Palo Alto, Calif.: Science and Behavior Books, 1972), pp. 20-79.

11. Murray Bowen, *Family Therapy in Clinical Practice* (New York: Jason Aronson, 1978), pp. 529-47.

12. Satir, *Conjoint Family Therapy*, p. 82.

13. Minuchin, *Families of the Slums*, p. 198.

14. Nathan W. Ackerman, *The Psychodynamics of Family Life* (New York: Basic Books, 1958), p. 53.

15. Salvador Minuchin develops this theory in *Families and Family Therapy*, pp. 51-55.

CHAPTER 7: MARRIAGE AND FAMILY

1. Robert Carkhuff and Bernard Berenson, *Beyond Counseling and Therapy* (New York: Holt, Rinehart & Winston, 1967). Here he emphasizes, throughout the book, counseling as a way of life.

2. Charles Stewart, *The Minister as Family Counselor* (Nashville: Abingdon, 1979), p. 22.

3. Robert M. Simon, "Sculpting the Family," *Family Process*, vol. 11 (March 1972), pp. 49-57.

4. Vincent Foley, *An Introduction to Family Therapy* (New York: Grune and Stratton, 1974), p. 117.

5. Murray Bowen, *Family Therapy in Clinical Practice* (New York: Jason Aronson, 1978), p. 540.

6. Details concerning the problem-solving approach to family counseling can be found in Jay Haley, *Problem Solving Therapy* (Washington: Jossey Bass, 1979).

7. Many of the details of what takes place in the first interviews and in contracting are not included here. See Haley, *Problem Solving Therapy*, pp. 9-47, for further details about this subject.

CHAPTER 8: NURTURING IMAGES

1. Don S. Browning, *The Moral Context of Pastoral Care* (Philadelphia: Westminster Press, 1976), pp. 104-15.

2. Carl Jung in *Symbols of Transformation* (Princeton: Princeton University Press, 1976), draws a parallel between regression in emotional difficulty and in symbol formation. See chapter 3, "The Transformation of Libido," and chapter 5, "Symbols of the Mother and of Rebirth."

3. Psychoanalysis refers to long-term counseling where the inner conflict of the client is the focus, and skillful use is made of transference and counter-transference.

4. Carl Jung, *The Practice of Psychotherapy* (New York: Bollingen Series XX, Pantheon Books, 1966), p. 147.

5. For distinction between brief forms of counseling and extended counseling, see Seward Hiltner, *Pastoral Counseling* (Nashville: Abingdon Press, 1949), pp. 80-94.

6. Robert R. Carkhuff and Bernard G. Berenson, *Beyond Counseling and Therapy* (New York: Rinehart & Winston, 1967), p. 27.

7. *Ibid.*

8. *Ibid.*, pp. 28 and 29.

9. David W. Allen, "Basic Treatment Issues" in *Hysterical Personality*, Mardi J. Horowitz, ed. (New York: Jason Aronson, 1977), p. 296.

10. Jung, *The Practice of Psychotherapy*, p. 147.

11. Transference resistance and transference compliance are projections onto the therapeutic relationship of frustrating relationships of one's past. They both are forms of controlling internal object relationships. The internal objects are controlled by either resisting or complying to therapeutic treatment. In either case, the resistance or compliance is the result of transference distortion.

12. Jung, *The Practice of Psychotherapy*, p. 147.

13. Carl G. Jung, *Archetypes of the Collective Unconscious* (Princeton: Princeton University Press, 1959), p. 26.

14. *Ibid.*, p. 31.

15. *Ibid.*, p. 8.

CHAPTER 9: IMAGE EXPLORATION

1. Berger, *Facing Up to Modernity*, p. 6.

2. *Ibid.*, p. 11.

3. Here I diverge from Peter Berger. He believes all views of reality are socially constructed. See Peter Berger and Thomas Luckmann, *The Social Construction of Reality* (Garden City, N.Y.: Archer Books, 1966).

4. Berger, *Facing Up to Modernity*, p. 11.

5. *Ibid.*, p. 16.

6. Murray Bowen, *Family Therapy in Clinical Practice* (New York: Jason Aronson, 1978), pp. 248-50. Bowen defines this approach to couple therapy in detail.